Laughter
Ever After...

Other Books by Donald Capps

*Fragile Connections: Memoirs of Mental Illness
for Pastoral Care Professionals*

Giving Counsel: A Minister's Guidebook

Jesus: A Psychological Biography

Social Phobia: Alleviating Anxiety in an Age of Self-Promotion

With Gene Fowler
The Pastoral Care Case: Learning about Care in Congregations

Edited by Donald Capps
Re-Calling Ministry by James E. Dittes

Laughter
Ever After...
Ministry of Good Humor

DONALD CAPPS

CHALICE
PRESS

ST. LOUIS, MISSOURI

Cover image: Elizabeth Wright, using images from FotoSearch
Cover and interior design: Elizabeth Wright

Visit Chalice Press on the World Wide Web at
www.chalicepress.com

10 9 8 7 6 5 4 3 2 1   08 09 10 11 12

Library of Congress Cataloging-in-Publication Data
Capps, Donald.
    Laughter ever after : ministry of good humor / Donald Capps.
      p. cm.
    ISBN 978-0-8272-2141-3
    1. Wit and humor—Religious aspects—Christianity. I. Title.
    BR115.H84C37 2008
    248.402'07—dc22

                            2007050022

Printed in United States of America

To Eamon August
Welcome!

Contents

Acknowledgments

I want to thank Trent Butler for his steady encouragement, Pablo A. Jiménez for his expert copyediting and attention to details, and the rest of the staff at Chalice Press, especially Lisa Scronce and Cindy Meilink, for all of the hard work and dedication that go into the production and marketing of a book. I have been extremely fortunate to have several of my books published by Chalice Press. Because of Chalice Press, and my earlier association with The Graduate Seminary of Phillips University, I feel that I am a honorary member of the Disciples of Christ and a follower in the footsteps of Alexander Campbell. I am also indebted to Sang Uk Lee for helping me track down books and articles on humor, and to Harry Freebairn, who, until his retirement as director of field education at Princeton Theological Seminary, was a continuing source of jokes, puns, and cartoons.

This book was written as my wife, Karen, and I were eagerly anticipating the arrival of our first grandchild. The fact that these two gestation processes were going on simultaneously has taught me that it's impossible to compete with a baby as far as attention and excitement are concerned, but fortunately I knew this from having observed a great many infant baptisms in my day. (O.K., I may have exaggerated my credentials as a follower of Alexander Campbell in the previous paragraph.) Who, after all, pays any attention to the minister or even the doting parents? So I had little choice but to dedicate this book to Eamon August, and to extend him a heartfelt welcome to the world. Given that this is a first for our son, John, I thought he might appreciate some fatherly support as the birth approached, so I shared with him the following jokes:

A man speaks frantically into the phone, "My wife is pregnant and her contractions are only two minutes apart!" "Is this her first child?" the doctor queries. "Don't be silly!" the man shouts, "This is her husband!"

A young couple was nervously expecting their first baby. As her contractions began in earnest, the wife calmly announced to her husband that it was time to get to the hospital. Noting that it was rush hour, he shouted as he ran out the door ahead of her, "Let's take both cars. That way, one of us is sure to make it in time."

I thought he would appreciate these words of support, but I should have known, as a rather experienced "Minister of Good Humor," that not everyone is ready to hear the gospel at the time it is preached. But not to despair. They may come around later and tell you that your words were not wasted, after all.

Preface

The idea of this book is that any Christian person of any age or station in life can minister to others by understanding the strengths and the limits of humor: what it can do for us, and what we should not expect it to do. Humor can be a wonderful resource for enabling us to get along better than we do, for helping us get through difficult times in life, for helping us appreciate the life that God has given us. Because it *is* such a wonderful resource, we may be tempted to abuse it, exploit it, or treat it as a panacea for difficulties and problems it is not meant or designed for. Like any*thing* we cherish in life, we need to treat humor with respect; like any*one* we cherish in life, we need to treat humor lovingly, with generosity, goodwill, and grace, and it will respond in kind.

This book is intended to help those who want to be Ministers of Good Humor to know something about the real, proven benefits of humor, who want to participate in the creation of a good humor ethos, who want to know about the human needs to which humor can sensitize us, who want to understand what humor has to offer those who are trying to cope with aging, illness, and death, and who want to know the qualities that are likely to enable one to be an effective Minister of Good Humor.

I invite readers of this book to think of it as a Ministry of Good Humor handbook. *Webster's New World College Dictionary* defines a handbook as "a compact reference book on some subject; manual of facts or instructions."[1] It is not an exhaustive treatment of the subject, but it should be enough to get readers started on the Ministry of Good Humor. Some people are already on the way. Some have been doing it for so long it has become second nature. They are so good at it that they probably don't need this book. But they might want to share it with a friend who seems like a person who would be an excellent Minister of Good Humor, but needs a little encouragement. This book could also be the textbook for a Ministry of Good Humor class. The chapters are probably brief enough so that the class could cover one chapter per week, and members who attend all or most of the class meetings would receive a Minister of Good Humor badge or certificate at the end of the course. If they apply their knowledge outside of the classroom, I can virtually guarantee that they will make a difference in other people's lives and they will gain some valuable insights into themselves as well.

Most of the teachers whom I know like to explain in understandable terms what the course is about. When I do this, I try to define the key terms—in this case, *ministry, good,* and *humor*—and I make a bee line for the dictionary so that no one will accuse me of beginning a course with a personal bias. The dictionary defines *ministry* as "the act of ministering, or serving."[2] Not much help there, so let's go to the word *minister.* There are lots of meanings for this word. The most relevant are "a person acting for another as agent," and "the agent of some power, force, etc. (such as a *minister* of evil)."[3] So, as Christians, we act as agents for our Lord Jesus, and because he is good, we are ministers of *good,* not evil.

So what does *good* mean? There are seventeen definitions of the word *good.* These are the most relevant: "valid, genuine, real (as in *good* money or a *good* excuse)," "healthy, strong, vigorous (as in *good* eyesight)," "enjoyable, desirable, pleasant, happy, etc. (as in a *good* life)," and "dependable, reliable, right (as in *good* advice)."[4] There is also "proper, becoming, correct (as in *good* manners),"[5] but I sort of resist this one, because good humor usually walks the rather narrow pathway between being proper on the one hand and giving offense on the other. So let's flag that issue and move on to *humor.*

Humor is "the quality that makes something seem funny, amusing, or ludicrous" and "the ability to perceive, appreciate, or express what is funny, amusing, or ludicrous."[6] So what does *funny* mean? *Funny* is "the simple, general term for anything that excites laughter or mirth."[7] I think we all know what laughter is. *Mirth* is "joyfulness, gaiety, or merriment, especially when characterized by laughter."[8]

So what do we have? Or, better, who are we? We are agents for the Lord Jesus who serve him by promoting laughter, amusement, joyfulness, gaiety, and merriment that is valid, genuine, and real; healthy, strong, and vigorous; enjoyable, pleasant, desirable, and happy; dependable, reliable, and right! Not bad for starters. Climb aboard the Happy Special. It's over on the Sunshine Track.

Get a Transfer

If you are on the Gloomy Line,
Get a transfer.
If you're inclined to fret and pine,
Get a transfer.
Get off the track of doubt and gloom,
Get on the Sunshine Track—there's room—
Get a transfer.
If you're on the Worry Train,
Get a transfer.
You must not stay there and complain,
Get a transfer.
The Cheerful Cars are passing through,
And there's lots of room for you—
Get a transfer.
If you're on the Grouchy Track,
Get a transfer.
Just take a Happy Special back,
Get a transfer.
Jump on the train and pull the rope,
That lands you at the station Hope—
Get a transfer.[9]

So where are we going?

The Town of Don't You Worry

There's a town called Don't-You-Worry
On the banks of River Smile;
Where the Cheer-up and Be-happy
Blossom sweetly all the while.
Where the Never-Grumble flower
Blooms beside the fragrant Try,
And the Ne'er-Give-Up and Patience
Point their faces to the sky.
In the valley of Contentment
In the province of I-Will,
You will find this lovely city,
At the foot of No-Fret Hill.
There are thoroughfares delightful
In this very charming town,
And on every hand are shade trees
Named the Very-Seldom-Frown.
Rustic benches quite enticing,
You'll find scattered here and there,
And to each a vine is clinging
Called the Frequent-Earnest prayer.
Everybody there is happy,
And is singing all the while,
In the town of Don't-You-Worry
On the banks of River Smile.[10]

Too good to be true? Not if the Lord's Ministers of Good Humor are afoot.

1

What Good Is Humor?

If you want to be a Minister of Good Humor, you'll want to know the benefits of humor and to tell other people what it's good for. Some skeptics think it's a waste of time, that it's frivolous, pointless, a distraction from what's important. You'll want to be able to answer the skeptics. This chapter tells you how to do this. It does this by reporting on empirical studies that have proven that humor has some real benefits. So if some skeptics say to you, "The last thing we need around here is a Minister of Good Humor," you can refer to this handbook and say, in an appropriately authoritative tone of voice, "With all due respect, studies show…" If they are fair-minded, they will say, "You've convinced us," and allow you to go about your business. You may even have converted *them* to the gospel of Good Humor.

On the other side of the argument are the folks who, like myself, grew up with *The Reader's Digest* view that "laughter is the best medicine." This belief goes all the way back to the Bible: "A cheerful ["merry" in KJV] heart is a good medicine; but a downcast spirit dries up the bones" (Prov. 17:22 NRSV). The folks who take this position would seem to be your best allies, but, as Robert R. Provine points out in his book *Laughter: A Scientific Investigation*,[1] many of the claims for the medicinal or health-promoting nature of laughter and humor are pretty exaggerated. So, if you are to be a Minister of *Good* Humor in the "valid, genuine, real" sense of *good*, you will not want to cozy up with the "laughter is good for your health" crowd. The best strategy for the promotion of good humor is to lay out a middle way between the skeptics and the enthusiasts.

The Overselling of the Health Benefits of Laughter and Humor

The idea that laughter is the best medicine got a big shot in the arm when Norman Cousins wrote about his affliction with a painful and life-threatening degenerative disease (ankylosing spondylitis) and his successful self-treatment with vitamin C, Marx Brothers' movies, and episodes from the television series *Candid Camera*. In collaboration with his physician, he removed himself from the hospital and checked into a hotel, where he improvised a therapeutic regime that included a healthy dose of humor. In a 1976 article published in the prestigious *New England Journal of Medicine*, expanded into a book titled *The Anatomy of an Illness as Perceived by the Patient*,[2] he claimed that ten minutes of laughter provided him at least two precious hours of pain-free sleep and other desirable health benefits. His book became a best seller and he became a widely sought speaker on medical matters from the patient's perspective. Later in life he moderated his laugh-your-way-to health message, noting that humor should be thought of as a metaphor for the entire range of positive emotions. But the idea that laughter was the key factor in the remission of his disease is what everyone seems to remember, and other explanations have been conveniently set aside. There is something about the scene of a man sitting in his hotel bed watching videos and laughing his head off and getting well that has almost universal appeal.

Provine doesn't want to expunge this picture completely from our minds, but he says that studies of the physiological effects of laughter haven't proven much of anything. After reviewing a lot of them, Provine concludes: "No amount of scholarship can piece together a coherent physiological picture of laughter or humor from this hodgepodge of odd parts. Investigators often disagree about the most basic results."[3] He points out that in none of these studies was there a control for the possibility that the presumed effects of laughter were really due to the playful social settings in which laughter occurred, not from laughing itself. No study evaluated the uniqueness of laughter's physiological profile by contrasting it with other energetic vocalizations like shouting or cheering.

Then what about longevity? Does a "cheerful heart" add years to your life? Unfortunately, a study of the long-term effects of personality on health actually showed that cheerfulness (optimism and sense of humor) in childhood was *inversely* related to longevity. A better predictor of a long life was conscientiousness.

The authors of this study suggested "to the extent that optimism and humor are healthy, they may act as adaptive coping mechanism to a transient crisis."[4] Provine shares this view, noting that there is "little scientific support for the popular idea that people with the personality traits of humor, cheerfulness, or optimism are particularly healthy or long-lived, but the possibility remains that situational laughter and humor are effective coping mechanism for transient stress."[5] In other words, if a cheerful heart is a good medicine, it's a medicine that works like a placebo—it probably doesn't have any physiological benefits, but it does seem to have psychological benefits.

So what are these psychological benefits? Having combed through scores of empirical studies on the psychological benefits of humor, I believe that humor has three main benefits: it may help to reduce life-stress; it may help to alleviate milder forms of depression; and it may help to reduce anxiety. A related conviction is that the person with a well-developed "sense of humor" is more likely to experience these benefits than a humorless person who has sporadic bursts of humor. But measuring a "sense of humor" empirically is problematic, especially because the studies suggest that there are two ways to be a humor-loving person: you can be a person who produces humor for others to enjoy, and you can be a person who enjoys the humor produced by others. This means that you can have a well-developed sense of humor and never tell a joke or even say something funny or comical with a group of friends. In fact, your sense of humor may be more well-developed than a person who is constantly saying funny things or performing amusing antics. With these preliminary thoughts out of the way, let's take a look at the empirical studies. In presenting them, I will do my best to make them as nontechnical and palatable as I can. I wouldn't want to turn off any readers in the very first chapter. On the other hand, if you have an aversion to empirical psychology, no one is compelling you to hang around. Take a breather, and let's get together again at the beginning of chapter 2.

Humor Reduces Life-Stress

"Doctor, you gotta help me. I'm under so much stress that I keep losing my temper."

"Just calm yourself, and tell me all about it."

"I JUST DID, YOU STUPID IDIOT!"

Almost everyone agrees that stress is greater today than at any time in our nation's history. In our grandparents' and parents' generations, people complained of chronic fatigue.[6] Today, we complain of stress and being "stressed out." When our grandparents and parents talked about stress, they were usually talking about the structures of buildings, and whether a post or wall could handle the weight placed upon it. In much the same way, we talk about the pressure we feel, the strain we are under, the tension in our minds and bodies. When we think of ways to reduce pressure, tension, and strain, we might not think of humor because humor seems so temporary and fleeting. This, to some extent, is true. What reduces life-stress most is not an occasional joke but a sense of humor, or a humorous temperament or disposition. However, a sense of humor can be cultivated or nurtured. It's the rare baby who comes laughing through the birth canal and has a ready smile for the obstetrician. Most looked scared, confused—stressed out. So, if we are not born with a sense of humor, we can develop it, and it's never too late to get on with it.

But what's the evidence that humor reduces life-stress? The study of the link between humor and stress reduction has been going on for forty years. It began when a psychology professor, Herbert Lefcourt, a psychology professor at the University of Waterloo in Ontario, Canada, had a couple of students who, under his advisement, wrote their doctoral dissertations on humor.[7] Humor research ended when both of them graduated. But then Lefcourt attended his father's funeral. He expected a very solemn occasion. Instead, the reuniting of family members far and wide was an occasion for mirth and good will. This was not at all out of disrespect for his father. It was almost in his honor. He had always been ready to make light of the grimmest of circumstances, often with a joke or cliché that would fit the occasion and cause others to take the situation less seriously. The humor displayed at the funeral was very much in character with the ways his father would have joked if he had been there to take part.

Lefcourt's experience at his father's funeral led him to begin studying humor in earnest, and he and Rod Martin, a fellow Canadian teaching psychology at the University of Western Ontario, developed a humor questionnaire. It was designed to measure the propensity to smile or laugh in a variety of daily life situations, the kinds of situations that are likely to cause a person to get embarrassed, irritated, upset, or angry. A typical question is, "Suppose you were eating in a restaurant with some friends and the waiter accidentally spilled a drink on you." The choices range from "I would not have found this particularly amusing" to "I would have laughed heartily at my own expense." (Maybe the question should have specified whether the drink was hot or cold; almost everyone I have discussed this question with has said if the drink was hot, they would howl in pain.) Then they developed a coping humor scale consisting of seven statements that would ask you to rate your degree of agreement or disagreement. Typical statements include, "I usually look for something comical to say when I am in tense situations," or, "I must admit that my life would probably be easier if I had more of a sense of humor."

The idea was to use both instruments to find out if a sense of humor reduced life-stress. They also used a questionnaire to assess a person's current mood level, with five negative moods—including tension, depression, anger, fatigue, and confusion—and one positive mood—vigor. Every study that Lefcourt and Martin carried out had the same result: humor reduced the impact of stress.   No gender differences were found. A study of severely disabled persons had the same result. The authors found that there was greater acceptance or transcendence of their disabilities by those who were able to express humor about the very state of being disabled. The authors concluded that persons who are *not* disabled "have much to learn about humor and grace from handicapped persons."[8]

Studies by other researchers have supported these findings. In a study by Smadar Bizi, Giora Keinan, and Benjamin Beit-Hallahmi,[9] 159 Israeli soldiers, aged 19–20, who were taking part in a training course for combat and defense forces, filled out the questionnaires developed by Lefcourt and Martin. In addition, crew members evaluated one another on two kinds of humor: *productive* humor, when one tells jokes and makes humorous comments that cause others to smile or laugh; and *reactive* humor, when one mainly enjoys the jokes and humorous comments that others make. These researchers found that humor aided performance under stress, and that this was especially true for *productive* humor. They were not sure why it was more helpful for those who tell jokes and make humorous comments, but the probable explanation is that making light of the stressful situation is more likely to reduce their own inner stress and tension. Those who merely *react* with a smile or laughter to the jokes or humorous comments of others may not experience the same release.

Humor Moderates Mild Depression
A guy and his girlfriend were going out on the town. When he called for her at her tenth-story apartment, she wasn't quite ready. She said to make himself at home, so he began playing ball with her little dog.

The door to the balcony was open, and when the ball bounced out the door and over the ledge of the balcony, the dog leaped after it. A few minutes later his girlfriend appeared, looking as lovely as ever. He asked, "Have you noticed your dog has been acting depressed lately?"

By all accounts, depression has been on the increase over the past several decades. The American Psychiatric Association indicates that the lifetime risk for major depressive disorder in community samples has varied from 10 to 25 percent for women, and from 5 to 12 percent for men, and that the lifetime prevalence of chronic depression is 6 percent.[10] These numbers represent just a small percentage of the persons who experience less severe forms of depression that do not come to the attention of psychiatrists or psychotherapists. Also, many persons do not use the word *depression* to express how they feel. Instead, they may talk about being sad, discouraged, gloomy, or unhappy. Or they may be having trouble sleeping, or complain of listlessness, or have difficulty concentrating or making decisions, or have a low opinion of themselves, or have feelings of hopelessness, all of which are common symptoms of depression.[11]

Because humor is associated with mirth—joyfulness, gaiety, or merriment—it isn't surprising that researchers would try to find out if humor has an effect on depression. Because the studies by Lefcourt and Martin also found some evidence that humor moderates depression (one of the five negative moods that they studied), Albert Porterfield decided to test whether humor reduced depression as well as life-stress.[12] Surprisingly, he didn't find much evidence that humor reduced life-stress, but he did find considerable evidence that humor moderates depression. He guessed that stressful life experiences are typically the cause of depression, so the idea that humor reduces life-stress was indirectly supported.

A subsequent study by Stephanie L. Deaner and Jasmin T. McConatha came up with the opposite results. Humor helped persons cope with stressful situations but had less effect on depression.[13] If we compare the depression scores of the persons they studied with the persons who Porterfield studied, we can come up with a pretty good explanation for the difference. Porterfield's study used students at Oberlin College, and they had very high depression scores. Deaner and McConatha used students at West Chester University, and they had unexpectedly low depression scores. Their depression scores were probably less affected by humor because they were so low to begin with.

On the other hand, some students at West Chester University were more depressed than others. What Deaner and McConatha discovered was that those who were less depressed use humor as a coping mechanism more than those who were more depressed. This could explain why Porterfield didn't find much support for the idea that humor helps persons cope with life-stress. There may be a point where depression is so severe that humor is unable to moderate the stresses of life.

What these two studies seem to tell us is that the relationship between humor, depression, and coping with life-stresses is quite complex. Another team of researchers, Arthur M. Nezu, Christine M. Nezu, and Sonia E. Blissett,[14] studied a group of Fairleigh Dickinson University students, and found that humor moderated the depression scores of persons who were currently experiencing a stressful situation in their lives. This finding suggests that someone who is chronically depressed may not be helped by humor, but that humor may help someone who is currently having a rough time of it, and has gotten depressed as a result.

Humor Helps to Reduce Anxiety

An elderly woman was terrified of flying to visit her family in Australia, because she was so afraid that there would be a bomb on board. They tried to convince her that the risk of such an occurrence was remote and persuaded her to consult an actuary. "What are the chances of someone having a bomb on a plane?" she asked. "Very slight," he replied, "About one in 10,000." "And what are the chances of two people having a bomb on the same plane?" "Even smaller. Something like one in a billion. Practically zero." After that, she was happy to fly...as long as *she* took a bomb on board.

The fact that humor may reduce life-stress raises the question of whether it also helps with anxiety. Anxiety and stress are not the same thing, but they often overlap. The pressure, strain, or tension one feels when one is stressed may be due to anxiety. (It could also be due to fear.) Anxiety is a state of being uneasy, apprehensive, or worried about what may happen; it is a concern about a possible future event.[15] Psychiatrists refer to it as "anticipatory dread," especially dread of a situation in which we think we will be placed in a vulnerable position.[16] Our feelings of vulnerability may cause us to "catastrophize," or to dwell on the worst possible outcome.[17] "I will flunk the midterm and fail the course," "The plane will crash and everyone will survive but me," "My proposal of marriage will be flat-out rejected and, in my despair, I will jump off the nearest bridge."—that sort of thing.

Several years before Lefcourt and Martin studied the link between humor and life-stress, Ronald E. Smith and his colleagues tested some students at Purdue University to see if humor reduced their anxiety as they took an examination.[18] About half of the 215 students were given an examination that contained one-third humorously worded test items, and the other half received a nonhumorous form of the test. Several weeks prior to the exam, they filled out a test to determine their normal anxiety level (low, moderate, or high). When they took the examination, half of the high anxiety group was given the humorous exam, the other half was given the nonhumorous exam. The same was done with the moderate and the low anxiety groups.

So what happened? The test scores of the high anxiety / nonhumorous test group were much *lower* than the scores of both low anxiety groups and both moderate anxiety groups, and the test scores of the high anxiety / humorous test group were much higher, equaling the performance level of the other two anxiety groups. So, for the high anxiety group, humor obviously helped.

But something unexpected happened. The moderate anxiety/humorous test group performed at a rather low level on the test, even lower than the moderate anxiety/nonhumorous test group. Why didn't the humor help them? In talking with some of these students, the researchers found out that the humorous questions helped them "loosen up," but they also had a distracting effect.

What this study seems to show is that persons who are very anxious are especially likely to be helped by humor. This is the opposite of persons who are depressed. The more deeply depressed, the less likely humor will be of any assistance. This study also indicates what most persons who go in for humor are already aware of—that when they use humor to loosen others up, others may experience such efforts as an irritating distraction. The grade school class clown comes to mind. Maybe he was a high anxiety guy who did it mainly for his own benefit.

Another study had both an expected and an unexpected result. In a study conducted at Allegheny College by Nancy A. Yovetich, J. Alexander Dale, and Mary A. Hudak,[19] two groups of students awaited an anticipated application of an electric shock. The group who were shown some comedy routines had less anxiety than those presented with a geological documentary as they waited. While they awaited the shock, both groups were informed that the shock would cause no physical damage, but if they wished to discontinue the experiment, they should knock loudly on the instrument panel in front of them and the experiment would be terminated. They assumed that the shock, which was never applied, was to be the test. Little did they know that the test was going on as they anticipated the dreaded event. That those watching comedy had less anxiety was the expected outcome. The unexpected one was that the persons who benefited most were the ones who scored lower on a sense of humor test. One explanation is that persons with a greater sense of humor are more likely to be helped by *productive* than *reactive* humor. Still, this result left the researchers scratching their heads and wondering if the artificial conditions in which the students were placed had something to do with it.

At this point, I can well imagine that older readers of this little handbook may be saying to themselves, "Why don't these psychologists study the effect of humor on something that is really worth being anxious about? After all, midterm exams and even electric shocks are rather small potatoes as far as reasons to get anxious are concerned!" Fair enough. How's death for a potentially anxiety-provoking event? James Thorson, a gerontologist at the University of Nebraska in Omaha, and his colleague, F.C. Powell, tested the relationship between sense of humor and death anxiety.[20] They studied 426 persons (290 women, 136 men) ranging in age from 18 to 90, with a mean age of just under 38. They devised a sense of humor scale, which included coping humor, humor production, humor appreciation, and appreciation of humorous people. Only one of the four made a difference. Those who used coping humor *less* scored somewhat higher on the death anxiety scale.

There were some small differences between the women and the men. Women were slightly lower in humor production and slightly higher in their use of coping humor. Also, coping humor increased slightly as the age of the respondent increased. Older persons also showed a bit less appreciation of humor itself and a bit more appreciation of humorous people. It is worth noting that this study only involved filling out questionnaires. It did not include direct exposure to humor, such as jokes and cartoons, relating to death, a procedure that paid significant dividends for Lefcourt and Martin when they studied disabled persons.

One last study on the effects of humor on anxiety is one that I especially like. William E. Kelly, a member of the counseling department at the University of Nevada at Las Vegas, conducted an investigation of worry and sense of humor.[21] He used a worry questionnaire that assesses five areas of life in which a person might have worries, including personal relationships, lack of confidence, aimless future, work concerns, and financial concerns. (Incidentally, *Webster's New World College Dictionary* says that *worry* means "to feel distressed in the mind; be anxious, troubled, or uneasy"[22]). Kelly also used the sense of humor scale developed by Thorson and Powell to determine whether humor has any relationship with worry, and, if so, in what ways. As I have mentioned, the sense of humor scale includes humor production, humor as a means of coping, humor appreciation, and appreciation of humorous persons.

Kelly didn't try to guess what the results would be, but we probably should not be surprised to learn that there was a negative relationship between worry and sense of humor. In other words, persons with a high sense of humor are less likely to worry. The main reason for this, though, was that worry had a very negative effect on humor production. Because there was also a strong positive association between humor production and confidence, Kelly guesses that lack of confidence hinders persons from humor production. This may be because "worriers would question their ability to produce humor in such a way that others would find favorable."[23] A similar explanation might be made for the relationship Kelly found between worries about personal relationships and humor. He guesses that persons "who worry about disrupting, or losing, relationships might be less inclined to use humor for fear that others will not approve of their humor."[24]

The findings mentioned so far are pretty much along the lines that we would probably expect. There was one finding, though, that hardly anyone would have expected. I certainly would not have. This was the fact that worry was *positively* related to one of the humor dimensions—which was coping humor, or using humor to cope with frustrations and problems. This less surprised Kelly because he knew of another study that demonstrated that worry is an active cognitive coping mechanism. We tend to think that worry doesn't do any good, that, if anything, worrying makes things worse. But if humor helps people cope and worry helps people cope, "it is less surprising that worry and coping with humor are positively related."[25] These findings suggest that worriers are less likely to deal with negative life experiences by treating them lightly, as though they are not worth taking seriously, and more likely to employ humor as a way to mitigate the negative *consequences* or *outcomes* of these experiences. The startling conclusion, then, is that worry is a means to *reduce* anxiety and to *avoid* depression!

Worry and Humor: Partners in Coping

The Jewish mother's telegram: "Begin worrying. Details follow."

A popular song of the 1980s advised, "Don't worry, be happy." And the poem in the preface of this book says "There's a town called Don't-You-Worry / On the banks of River Smile." Kelly's study suggests, instead, that worry may actually contribute to happiness—the cheerful heart—by forestalling anxiety and depression. Since humor also has these effects, worry and humor have a lot more in common than we would have guessed. If anxiety relates to situations that we dread because we suspect that we will be vulnerable, worry and humor may be thought of as partners in forestalling or inhibiting anxiety. Instead of viewing worry and anxiety as the same thing (despite what the dictionary says), we should instead think of worry as the opponent of anxiety, just as humor is. The difference is that the worrier does this by *anticipating* all the things that could *possibly* go wrong, while the humorist does this by *minimizing* the importance or significance of what may *in fact* go wrong.

This conclusion is supported by Julie K. Norem's *The Positive Power of Negative Thinking.*[26] She contends that negative thinking is actually a positive coping strategy for some individuals. Where others tend to minimize what might go wrong when they invite a group of friends over for dinner, or when they organize a business conference, negative thinkers (what Kelly would call "worriers") think of all the things that might go awry and plan for these exigencies. If "non-worriers" say to them that their fears are groundless or that many of the things they worry might happen are only remotely possible, the worrier may not disagree, but will still maintain that it is best to anticipate *all* the things that might go wrong. Kelly's study suggests that dealing with worries about these exigencies and remote possibilities has the positive effect of reducing anxiety. Thus, worry and anxiety are two very different psychological phenomena.

This being the case, we should probably change the poem presented in the preface to "There's a town called Don't-Be-Anxious / on the banks of River Smile." You and I should also volunteer to join the next team of Bible translators on the day that they are trying to figure out how to translate Matthew 6:25. The *King James Version* has Jesus saying, "Therefore I say unto you, *take no thought for your life,* what ye shall eat, or what ye shall drink; nor yet for your body, what ye shall put on" (emphasis added). Later translators, in addition to wanting to get rid of the archaic-sounding "ye," must have figured that "take no thought" could be misunderstood to mean that you and I are not to engage in any future planning whatsoever. They may have been thinking, too, that if people really did this, their families would have to share the burden of supporting them the rest of their lives or get them married into a wealthy family . Billy Collins, former United States Poet Laureate, imagines such an untroubled soul in the following poem:[27]

The Life of Riley: A Definitive Biography

He was born one sunny Florida morning
and napped through most of his childhood.
He spent his adult life relaxing in beach chairs,
always a tropical drink in his hand.
He never had a job, a family or a sore throat.
He never mowed a lawn.
Passersby would always stop to remind him
whose life it was he was living.
He died in a hammock weighing a cloud.

Here, Collins portrays the proverbial "life of Riley," the fellow whom Americans, back in the 1920s, 30s, and 40s, loved to envy.[28] One hardworking soul envied him so much that he wrote a song about the fellow who "lived the life of Riley when Riley wasn't around" (eating his food, sleeping in his bed, driving his car, etc.).

The New Testament section of the *Revised Standard Version* of the Bible was copyrighted in 1946. I can imagine that its team of translators were concerned that the "take no thought for your life" phrase in the *King James Version* would be misconstrued as an endorsement of the life of Riley, so they had to find an alternative. They came up with, "Therefore I tell you, *do not be anxious about your life,* what you shall eat or what you shall drink, nor about your body, what you shall put on" (emphasis added).

When the *Revised Standard Version* was updated in 1989, the "shalls" were changed to "wills," and "anxious" was changed to "worry." Thus, the *New Revised Standard Version,* published in 1989, reads: "Therefore I tell you, *do not worry about your life,* what you will eat or what you will drink, or about your body, what you will wear" (emphasis added). The *New International Version,* copyrighted in 1973, also uses "worry": "There I tell you, *do not worry about your life,* what you will eat or drink; or about your body, what you will wear" (emphasis added). In the version I own, there is a heading above verses 25–34 that reads, "Do Not Worry."

Given all the other biblical passages that Christians struggle over, I'm guessing that I am a party of one when it comes to fretting over the change from *anxious* to *worry.* The humorist in me tells me not to worry about it, that it's no big deal. But the worrier in me responds, "It's a very important issue, and that's why I'm writing about it now in a book that is attempting to proselyte on humor's behalf!" The two of me will probably not settle the issue by reaching a compromise, but we will continue to live together amicably, and this makes my point: I urge anyone who aspires to be a "Minister of Good Humor" to treat the "Priests of Worry" with respect. If you do, there's a greater chance that they will respect you, especially if you tell them that you and they are fighting against two common enemies—demonic forces—who are formidable opponents: Anxiety and Depression. Tell them, too, that you know that their methods are different from yours, and yours from theirs, but that these are merely differences in strategy, not in goals. Remember that you do not have to *convert* the worriers to your side. You only need to get them to respect you, and the best way to do this is to demonstrate that you respect them. Above all, don't put them on the defensive, because this is what others have been doing to them all their lives, and their resentment is justified.

What about Gender Differences?

Probably because of the perception that boys tend to goof-off more than girls do in grade school, we tend to think that men go in for humor more than women do, and that women are generally more serious than men. So it's natural to ask if there were gender differences in the empirical studies reported here. In fact, few gender differences were found or reported. As I have mentioned, Thorson and Powell found that women were slightly lower in humor production and slightly higher in using humor to cope with situations. Another finding was Robert Provine's discovery that women laugh more than men do, on a roughly 5 to 4 ratio.[29] He thinks this is due to the fact that men feel good when they elicit laughter from women especially, so they work hard to make women laugh, which leads women to laugh more. But a woman colleague of his suggested a simpler explanation, that "in dealing with men, there is so much more to laugh at."[30]

I *did* locate a study, though, that tested the gender issue directly. Millicent Abel wanted to know how humor and gender interact in moderating stress and the physical symptoms that result from stress.[31] She asked 131 students (70 men, 61 women) at Western Carolina University to fill out the humor scale developed by Thorson and Powell (the one that tests for coping humor, humor production, appreciation of humor, and appreciation of humorous persons), a perceived stress scale, and the anxiety and somatization scales from a symptom checklist. The somatization scale measures distress associated with common physical symptoms such as headache, loss of energy, and muscle aches.

Abel found no significant gender differences on the measures of perceived stress, distress from anxiety, and sense of humor. But she did find a gender difference on the measure of distress from physical symptoms, with the women reporting more physical distress than men. What about the effect of humor on anxiety, stress, and distress relating to physical symptoms? She found that humor had a "buffering effect" on stress for both genders, but that it had a buffering effect against anxiety for men only. She also found that for both genders, humor moderated the relationship between stress and physical symptoms. Since the major difference between men and women related to the "buffering effect" of humor for anxiety in men, she suggests that men and women with a greater sense of humor may use similar adaptive coping strategies against distress caused by physical symptoms but different strategies in response to distress caused by anxiety: "Men may prefer humor as a more appropriate expression of emotions such as anxiety, *whereas self-disclosure may be the preferred and more acceptable mode of expression for women*" (emphasis added).[32] The idea that women are more likely to talk about their anxiety makes a lot of sense. On the other hand, the contrast that Abel draws between humor and self-disclosure reflects the popular view that humor is a mask—in this case, a means of masking one's anxiety—and is not itself self-disclosive. Maybe we need a further study along the very lines that Abel has set forth that addresses this very question—namely, do men use humor as an indirect way of disclosing to others that they are experiencing anxiety?

What Ministers of Good Humor Can Learn from These Studies

Let's see if I can summarize the main things that we can learn from these empirical studies. Because most of them were based on subjects who were mostly in their late teens and early twenties, we need to be cautious in generalizing their findings to other age groups. Also, the results of these studies are not uniform. Some are even contradictory. Still, taken as a whole, they support the idea that humor may help a person cope with negative life experiences and that humor may counter the tendency to become depressed when one is in the throes of a painful life experience. It is less helpful for persons who are chronically depressed or suffering from a major depressive disorder. Whether humor helps to relieve the anxiety that occurs when a person is anticipating a negative life experience and its consequences is less clear, but it does seem to reduce or moderate anxieties relating to one's loss of control or inability to determine what happens. This could help to explain why persons who are afflicted with the problems due to aging will often use humor.

The research also seems to suggest that other people are likely to take notice of those who "produce" humor and to assign them a higher "sense of humor" score, but persons tend to rate themselves as having a good sense of humor on the basis of their ability to appreciate the humor that others produce, and to perceive the humor in their own negative life experiences. Thus, persons use humor as a coping mechanism in various ways. Some of these are overt and easy to recognize—such as cracking jokes in dire situations—while others are more covert and harder for others to detect—such as laughing to oneself.

In a general sort of way, the empirical studies summarized here confirm what we already knew, or thought we knew, about humor. There are a few surprises, but, by and large, the studies confirm the popular opinion that humor can be beneficial for moderating the effects of negative life experiences and that, even if it is not a panacea, it has minimal negative side effects when used or resorted to in this regard. This is not to say that humor has no negative side effects whatsoever; this would be to disregard the whole issue of offensive humor, a topic that I discussed in *A Time to Laugh,*[33] and will therefore not discuss further in this book. If they *do* confirm popular opinion about humor, this gives the research studies greater, rather than lesser, credibility, because we would tend to distrust studies that run counter to everything that we understand about humor from personal experience.

Interestingly enough, one of the studies reported here quotes the first half of Proverbs 17:22—"A merry heart doeth good like a medicine" (KJV), thus implicitly linking its investigation to the Bible itself. Unfortunately, the second half of the proverb—"but a downcast spirit dries up the bones" (NRSV) was omitted, so the proverb's suggestion that humor and depression are negatively related was therefore lost. Nor did any of the studies presented here take up the issue of misplaced humor, a topic that Proverbs 26:18–19 invites us to consider: "Like a maniac who shoots deadly firebrands and arrows, / is the one who deceives a neighbor / and says, 'I am only joking!'" Even so, the citation of Proverbs 17:22a in a scientific research study on humor suggests that contemporary researchers on the psychological benefits of humor are in good company, and, in light of Robert Provine's cautionary note about making unsubstantiated claims for the positive *physiological* effects of laughter and humor, it is rather nice to see this quotation in an article that explores their *psychological* effects.

The Indirect Benefits of Humor

The studies that I have presented here focus on the direct effects of humor. I want to conclude this review of empirical studies on the benefits of humor by mentioning a study showing that the benefits of humor may be indirect—that is, the humor may be beneficial to persons other than the ones for whom it is intended. In their article, "Laughter in a Psychiatric Ward," Marc Gelkopf, Shulamith Kreitler, and Mircea Sigal report on their study of the potential therapeutic effects of humor on hospitalized patients suffering from schizophrenia.[34] They carried out an experiment involving thirty-four resident patients in two chronic schizophrenic wards. Over a three-month period, the patients in Ward A were exposed to seventy humorous movies, while patients in Ward B were exposed to seventy movies of different genres (action, romance, drama, and some comedies). The main positive effect of this barrage of humorous movies was that the patients in Ward A experienced a slight but statistically significant decrease in verbal hostility as this was perceived by members of the nursing staff. This was what the authors had hoped would happen.

But there was also an unexpected result that had never entered their minds: They found that patients who "had been exposed to humor experienced a higher level of social support from the staff."[35] They couldn't tell if this "increased experienced support from the staff" was initiated "by some humor-induced change in the patients or by some humor induced change in the staff."[36] Whatever the most likely explanation may be, the patients noticed the change and reported it.

The authors concluded, "The humorous films affected the staff to a larger extent than the patients," and, therefore, "It may be advisable to consider the possibility of affecting the patients by projecting humorous films *with the staff as the target population*" (emphasis added).[37] One could therefore imagine a second article by the authors in which the *staff* reports that the *patients* treated them better than they had in the past! But the more important point is that the nursing staff did a better job of *caring* for the patients because they had been exposed to some humor. It wasn't that they made any overt efforts to amuse the patients, such as by telling them jokes. No. It was that they simply did their jobs better than they had before.

What this means is that even though nothing overtly funny or amusing occurs in the interaction between the professional and those for whom the professional is expected to care about, the care recipients may, nonetheless, be the beneficiaries of humor. If one of the features of professional burnout is *depersonalization,* or "a negative, cynical, and impersonal attitude towards the people one works with,"[38] this unexpected finding of the study suggests that caregiving persons may find in humor a valuable resource for maintaining a positive, hopeful, and personal attitude toward the persons they work with (parishioners, patients, students, other staff members, employees, employers, etc.).

This effect of humor on the unknowing recipient suggests that the psychological benefits of humor are often indirect. Therefore, they are not always easy to detect or to demonstrate empirically. This does not mean, though, that they are any less real or any less powerful than, say, being whacked on the head with a brickbat, plummeting into an uncovered manhole, or suffering the effects of a gunpowder blast:

> Every Thanksgiving, the Martins had Grandpa and Grandma Martin over for dinner. Grandpa Martin liked his turkey and stuffing with lots of pepper. Millie Martin, their daughter-in-law, asked little

Willie Martin to go fetch the pepper from the kitchen cupboard. Willie rummaged through the cupboard and found a container he thought was pepper, and brought it to Grandpa Martin. The next day Millie Martin discovered little Willie Martin's mistake. He had brought Grandpa Martin an unmarked box of gunpowder. So, Phil Martin called his father and explained the mistake. "Well," Grandpa Martin replied, "I'm glad to find out what happened, because when we got home last night, I leaned over to tie my shoe and I accidentally shot the cat."

2

Creating a Good Humor
Ministry Ethos

"A Guy Goes into a Bar..."

What I tried to do in the chapter you have just read is to make the case that humor has some real, tangible benefits. It may not help produce miraculous cures, and it isn't likely to prolong your life, but it *can* reduce or moderate life-stress, anxiety, and milder forms of depression. It can also help people who are in positions in which their job is to care for or nurture others to treat these others in a more caring and thoughtful manner.

In this chapter, I want to build on what has been presented so far by focusing on the ethos that is conducive to the reduction of life-stress, anxiety, and milder forms of depression. *Webster's New World College Dictionary* notes that the word *ethos* means "disposition" or "character" in Greek, and defines it as "the characteristic and distinguishing attitudes, habits, beliefs, etc., of an individual or a group."[1] I believe that such an ethos can be created in virtually any context in which persons gather together. Group psychotherapy and support groups may be especially intentional about creating such an ethos, but I suspect that such groups would not be necessary if we were doing a better job of creating such an ethos in more natural settings. Although readers of this book may think especially of the church context—meaning the local congregation—in which such an ethos might be created, Good Humor Ministry need not be confined to the congregational context. If fact, if we are serious about the mission of the church in the world, it would be unfortunate if it *were* confined to the congregational setting. As John Wesley proclaimed, "The world is my parish."

To inform our discussion, I will rely heavily on the book by Albert Tapper and Peter Press titled *A Guy Goes into a Bar...*,[2] plus a few other sources. I will suggest that the ethos that "A guy goes into a bar..." jokes create or assume is the very ethos that Good Humor Ministry seeks to foster.

For the church setting, the minister is the bartender (and if there is a ministerial staff, they share the bartender role; after all, the bar is usually open more hours than a single bartender can handle). The lay members are the patrons, but they occasionally pitch in for the bartender, especially when he needs to go to the restroom or has to deal with a situation that requires his undivided attention. If these lay members have enlisted in the corps of the Ministers of Good Humor, they express their care and concern for the other patrons. Outside the church setting, the lay members try to simulate the ethos of the bar wherever they happen to be. So does the bartender. The idea is to spread the bar ethos wherever we can. This bar has no bars!

I know, of course, that there are reasons for Christians to avoid bars. After all, they deal in alcohol there, and alcohol abuse, like other forms of substance abuse, has been, and continues to be, responsible for a great deal of human misery. So much so that the Christian Temperance Movement of the late nineteenth and early twentieth centuries waged war against the taverns, and eventually secured an amendment (the eighteenth) to the United States Constitution in 1919 prohibiting the manufacture, transportation, and sale of alcoholic beverages. The amendment was subsequently reversed by another amendment (the twenty-first) in 1933.[3]

The prohibition movement inspired—and was inspired by—the poetry of the day. One of my favorites is "Come

Home, Father," by Henry Clay Work (1832–1884), a printer by trade, who had leanings toward prohibition and against slavery. "Come Home, Father" tells the tragic story of a daughter who goes into the bar to plead with her father to come home because her little brother is deathly ill.[4] It begins:

> Father, dear father, come home with me now!
> The clock in the steeple strikes one;
> You promised, dear father, that you would come
>   home,
> As soon as your day's work was done.
> Our fire has gone out, our house is all dark,
> And mother's been watching since tea,
> With poor brother Bennie so sick in her arms,
> And no one to help her but me.
> Come home, come home, come home,
> Please father, dear father, come home.

This verse is followed by a refrain in the voice of the poet:

> Here the sweet voice of the child,
> Which the night-winds repeat as they roam!
> Oh! Who could resist this most plaintive of pray'rs,
> "Please father, dear father, come home."

But he doesn't respond. The daughter returns when the clock steeple strikes two, informing dear father that Benny is worse, and has been calling for his father. She reports that Ma believes he will die, perhaps before the morning dawns, and she sent this message by way of his daughter, "Come quickly or he will be gone." The poet repeats his plea to the father to hear the sweet voice of the child, and the daughter returns when the clock in the steeple strikes three to report:

> The house is so lonely, the hours are so long
> For poor weeping mother and me.
> Yes, we are alone—poor Benny is dead,
> And gone with the angels of light,
> And these were the very last words that he said,
> "I want to kiss Papa goodnight."

> Come home, come home, come home,
> Please, father, dear father, come home.

The poem ends with the poet's refrain.

Most of the poems of the prohibition era focused on the family of the husband and father who stopped in the tavern after getting off work, but in "Out in the Cold" by the Reverend Dwight Williamson, it is the drunkard who freezes to death:[5]

> Out of the bar-room into the cold,
> Money all gone and manhood sold,
> The poor man, weary from hunger and sin,
> Breasted the storm with quivering chin;
> Only the storm with its specters was out,
> And the eddying snow went whirling about;
> No thought of the drunkard out in the cold,
> Out in the cold.

In "Come Home, Father," the time of the night is determined by the church steeple clock. "Out in the Cold" was written by a minister, who refers to the poor man's "hunger and sin," and employs the metaphor of "out in the cold," as though he is the lost sheep that Jesus, the Good Shepherd, would do everything in his power to bring back to the fold. The implication is that the church and the bar are competing for a man's very soul, and that the bar is the very den of iniquity.

This view was instilled in me at an early age when my mother told me the story of her Swedish immigrant father. He would stop at the bar in South Omaha, where they lived, on his way home from work, and would sometimes not return home until the children were all in bed. But one night, on his walk home, he encountered a Salvation Army Band, and because he was a trumpet player himself, he stopped to listen. When he arrived home, he told his wife that while listening to the band, he decided to turn his life around. A week or so later, he was killed at work in an explosion. His wife, my grandmother, took comfort in the fact that he had accepted the Lord Jesus before his tragic death. I chose not to be a drinker myself (though I have to confess that I wanted to ask my mother if my grandfather had returned to the bar the next evening, after listening to the band, to see if he could convert his friends).

With this personal history, why the analogy between the bar and the creation of a God Humor Ministry ethos? One reason is that I believe that these working men were more at home in a bar than they were in a church. In the bar they could relax, talk with their friends—or complete strangers—about their troubles, their hopes, and their dreams—or simply, as the saying went, "mope in their beer." Another reason is that the "A guy goes into a bar…" jokes portray a bar that we can imagine in our minds—not a bar of fast-paced living, of fancy drinks, television, and high-tech music, but a bar with a few stools, some tables and chairs, and a restroom down the hall. It is small enough and, let's face it, dull enough, that if a guy comes walking in with a hamster in his hand, everyone notices at once, and knows that for the next half-hour, they will be watching the hamster perform—singing, dancing, or demonstrating his knowledge of the latest political news. In recent times, the television show "Cheers" comes closest to portraying this bar, but because it was a television show, it was more finely scripted than the bar that the "A guy goes into a bar…" portrays.

Having studied Tapper and Press's *A Guy Goes into a Bar…* as though I were going to be tested on it in a no less fictional seminary course on The Devil and All His Works, I have reached the conclusion that these jokes identify three fundamental human needs: for attention, companionship, and sympathy. No doubt, other needs may prompt a guy to go into a bar. But these seem to be the primary ones, and the jokes simply take them for granted. They play with them, but they don't question, challenge, or even debate them. They are an integral part of the ethos of the fictional bar. Let's take a closer look at these needs and how they get expressed.

The Need for Attention

Webster's New World College Dictionary has several definitions of attention, ranging from "thoughtful consideration for others" to "the erect, motionless posture of soldiers in readiness for another command," but the one most relevant here is "notice or observation (her smile caught my attention)."[6] For most of us, our need for attention is *not* insatiable. We can go for hours, even days, without expecting or seeking the attention of others. Some of us—those who are especially shy—actually try *not* to be noticed because being noticed is embarrassing and even creates discomfort.

I wrote about some of these persons in my book, *Social Phobia: Alleviating Anxiety in an Age of Self-Promotion.*[7] I told about one man who was shy and nervous around people—at work, in public, at church. As most shy persons feel that their true gifts go unrecognized because they are not more outgoing, he sought professional help. When the therapist discovered that he went to church every Sunday and sat in the back row, he set the man a goal: each week he was to sit in the pew in front of the one he sat in the previous week. Finally, in four or five months' time, he was sitting in the front pew. Not surprisingly, he found that people paid a lot more attention to him when he sat in the front pew. They esteemed him more highly. When I first read about this man, I found myself wishing that the therapist had assigned him the task of joining the choir! But, on second thought, having heard a lot of stories about church choirs and their internal conflicts, I was glad that the therapist left well enough alone. I also guessed that the man probably decided he was most comfortable sitting in a pew about halfway between the front and the back of the church.

Sooner or later, there is something inside of all of us that says, "I want others to notice me. I want them to take their eyes off others or the mirror on the wall and pay some attention, however fleeting, to me." Maybe this voice inside of us goes back to when we were babies and our mothers came in the room in the morning and greeted us with a cheery hello. The psychoanalyst Erik H. Erikson made a big point of this "greeting ceremony" between mother and infant, even going so far as to suggest that our desire to be recognized by God—to be lifted up and called by name—has roots in this experience.[8] As the benediction expresses it, "The LORD bless you and keep you. / The LORD make his face to shine upon you, and be gracious to you; / The LORD lift up his countenance upon you, and give you peace" (Num. 6:24-26).

If this need has roots in infancy, it gets further reinforcement in preschool and grade school, where other kids are vying for the teacher's attention. Some of us kids needed attention so much that we were willing to misbehave in order to get it. Others of us discovered that we could get attention—without detention—by becoming the class clown. No doubt, we all emerge from grade school with attention deficits that will take a lifetime to make up for.

In a certain sense, the bar is like a grade school classroom: you can get attention through misbehavior, but if you do, you risk being tossed out on your ear. If, instead, you do something funny or amusing, or come in with a prop (a frog that can dance, a dog that speaks the English language, etc.), most everyone in the bar will sit up and take notice, and if you play your cards right, you will also impress the bartender and maybe get a couple of free drinks for doing so. If you are prompted to say, "Then this implies that the need for attention is preadolescent, if not infantile," you won't get an argument from me. But this doesn't make the need itself any less genuine or the attentions we do receive any less welcome.

Here's a typical joke that illustrates this need. It's about a guy who doesn't make a very good initial impression when he goes into a bar. Fortunately for him, he has a hamster and a frog:

> A guy goes into a bar smelling and looking as if he hasn't had a bath in months. He orders a beer, but the bartender refuses: "I don't think you can pay for it." The guy says, "You're right. I haven't got any money, but if I show you something you've never seen before, will you give me a beer?" The bartender agrees. The guy pulls a hamster out of his coat pocket. He puts the hamster on the bar and it runs to the end of the bar, across the room, up to the piano, and onto the keyboard and begins playing Gershwin.

The bartender says, "You're right. I've never seen anything like that before. I'm really impressed. Here's your free beer." The guy downs his beer, and asks for another, suggesting the same deal as before. The bartender agrees. He reaches into his coat and this time pulls out a frog. He puts the frog on the bar and the frog begins to sing. He has a marvelous voice and great pitch. A stranger from the other end of the bar runs over to the guy and offers him $300 for the frog. "It's a deal," the guy says, and he takes the $300 and gives the stranger the frog. The stranger runs out of the bar. The bartender says to the guy, "Are you some kind of a nut? You sold a singing frog for $300? He's got to be worth millions. You must be crazy." "Don't worry," the guy replies, "the hamster is also a ventriloquist."

Notice that in these attention-getting jokes, the guy himself is rather nondescript. We assume that he doesn't attract much attention anywhere he happens to be, whether at work, at home, a shopping mall, wherever. If he entered the bar without an attention-attracting gimmick, he might be ignored there as well. But he invariably attracts the attention of the bartender and, once he gets the bartender's attention, he is likely to be recognized by the other patrons as well.

A guy who goes into a bar with a pet octopus is bound to attract attention, especially if the octopus has impressive musical skills:

A guy goes into a bar with his pet octopus, sets him up on the bar and says, "I bet anyone in here fifty bucks that my octopus can play any musical instrument you hand him." One guy walks up with a guitar and says, "You're on." He lays his fifty bucks on the bar, and hands over the guitar. The octopus proceeds to tune the strings and begins to play a wonderful rendition of Beethoven's "Moonlight Sonata." Everyone's aghast! The guy collects his fifty bucks. The next guy brings up a trumpet and lays his money on the bar. The octopus takes it, plays with the valves for a moment, then proceeds to imitate Louis Armstrong playing "Hello, Dolly." The guy collects his money again. The bartender leaves and comes back a few minutes later with a set of bagpipes and lays his fifty bucks on the bar. The octopus picks it up, turns it around, looks at it some more, turns it over again to get a different perspective. After a few minutes of this the bartender is getting impatient and asks, "What is he waiting for? Why doesn't he start playing?" The guy looks over and says, "Play it? He's trying to figure out how to get her pajamas off!"

This guy, too, got the attention of everyone in the bar because he didn't come in empty-handed. Moreover, he knows the octopus, which enables him to explain why the creature was able to handle the first two challenges with ease but is struggling with the third. It wasn't because the octopus wouldn't be able to play a Scottish jig once he figured out how to get the bagpipes into a playable position.

It occurred to me that these attention-getting jokes might be adult versions of "Show and Tell," a preschool and grade school activity in which a child brings in an object of interest, shows it to the class, and talks about it. My wife, who has taught preschool for many years, has given me some insights into "Show and Tell." One is that if the children are asked to bring in a book, they do so, but they bring along another object too. Some hide the object from the other children and only reveal it when it's their time to show it, though some may give their special friends a little glimpse of it beforehand. If they show a book, they want to build suspense by concealing its contents from the other kids. Some children who would be arriving late to class for another reason would delay their arrival even longer because they were searching around at home for the perfect object to bring with them so that they could use it to gain access to the small groups that they knew would already have formed without them. Of course, when the children were "on"—the child who was showing and telling—they seemed to want this moment when all eyes were on them to last forever. My wife guesses that being the center of attention and being in control would often go hand-in-hand. But most of all, there is a strong need to attract the attention of others as a vital step toward the sense of belonging.

How often do we hear someone saying that he or she went to so-and-so church, and "no one paid any attention to me." "A guy goes into a bar..." jokes suggest that receiving attention is a basic human need. They also suggest that some of us will go to rather extraordinary lengths to receive it, not because it is necessarily an end in itself—for such attention may be fleeting—but as the initial step toward gaining the sense that we are part of the group; that, before long, as the theme song of "Cheers" suggests, everyone will come to know our names. Here's a story in which a guy doesn't have to make an effort to gain attention. Instead, others have planned a party in his honor:

> A guy goes into a bar that he had frequented daily for the last sixty years. It was his ninetieth birthday, so the bartender and his friends decided to surprise him. They wheeled in a big birthday cake and out popped a beautiful young woman who said, "Hi, I can give you some super sex!" And the old man said, "Well, I guess I'll take the soup."

We *could* say that it took the bartender and his friends so long to get around to giving the man some much-deserved attention that it was too late. But that seems too cynical to me. Instead, the very nature of the attention they paid to him suggests that they hadn't written him off despite his advanced age. Where else but in a fictional bar does a ninety-year-old guy get *that* kind of recognition from his friends?

The Need for Companionship

Webster's New World College Dictionary says that a companion is "a person who associates with or accompanies another or others," and uses the words *sociable* and *fellowship* to indicate what companionship is about. The Latin word for *companion* literally means "bread fellow."[9] "Drinking buddy" has much the same meaning.

Most of us are around people much of our waking hours. In our dreams, we are often in a crowd of people, and, typically, a lot of them we've never seen before. So it isn't as though we live in total isolation. Even monks and nuns who have withdrawn from society live in monasteries and convents with other monks and nuns. But being around people is not the same as companionship. In fact, being around people makes us aware of our need for real companionship. Robinson Crusoe found companionship because there was one other man—Friday—on his isolated island. For Crusoe, it took only one to satisfy his need for companionship.

In 1950, David Riesman, in collaboration with Reuel Denney and Nathan Glazer, published a book titled *The Lonely Crowd: A Study of the Changing American Character.*[10] The sheer size of the book (almost 400 pages) was daunting for all but the most dedicated reader, but its title—"the lonely crowd"—was immediately embraced by thousands who had never read or even laid eyes on the book. I think that the title and much of its contents are still relevant today. Riesman suggests that earlier generations of Americans were "inner-directed" because their character was implanted early in life by their elders and was directed toward generalized but nonetheless inescapably destined goals. "Inner-directed" persons needed to develop the ability to maintain a delicate balance between the demands placed on them by their life goals and the buffetings of their external environment.[11]

Riesman contends that the "inner-directed" type was very much in decline, and was being replaced by the "other-directed" type. "Other-directed" persons are those for whom their own contemporaries are the source of direction in their lives. By "contemporaries," Riesman means either other persons who are known to the person or those with whom one is indirectly acquainted, through friends and the mass media. The goals toward which one is directed shift with the guidance provided by one's contemporaries. What remains constant is the process of paying close attention to the signals from others that enable one to set and alter one's life course.[12]

Riesman adds that "inner-directed" persons are prone to experience *guilt* when they do not live up to their destined goals, while "other-directed" persons are prone to experience a diffuse sense of *anxiety* as they struggle to find or discover the guidance they need from the myriad signals they are receiving from day to day and week to week.

To provide concrete images of the difference between these two types, for the "inner-directed" type, Riesman suggests the image of the *gyroscope*, "which is set going by parents and can receive signals later on from other authorities who resemble his parents."[13] I think, though, that the image of a *compass* does a better job of expressing the idea that the source of *direction* is implanted early in life. So I would suggest that we view the "inner-directed" as being given a compass at birth, one to which they may refer throughout their lives so that they do not stray from the path and lose their direction. I read John Bunyan's *The Pilgrim's Progress*[14] when I was a boy. The name of the hero of the book was Christian, so I identified with him. He knew that the path he was on led finally to the Celestial City. He met with many "buffetings" from his external environment—the temptations of Vanity Fair, imprisonment in Doubting Castle—but he had two companions who accompanied him—Faithful for the first half of the journey, Hopeful for the second—and these companionships made a world of difference. When Christian, nearing the completion of his journey, was crossing the River Jordan, he began to sink, but Hopeful held his head above water until his feet were on solid ground. Christian was an "inner-directed" type, but, just the same, he could have gotten lost if he didn't have these two good companions.

For the "other-directed" type, Riesman suggests the image of *radar*, which played a hugely important role in World War II. It now brings to mind air traffic controllers' difficult job of tracking the planes in the sky from the screen in front of them. Given the technological developments—both visual and auditory—that we have witnessed since Riesman's book was published, and the likelihood of many more, the radar image may seem rather obsolete. This, of course, would support his point that "other-directed" persons can ill-afford *not* to be aware of and able to use the latest technologies for tracking the very signals that provide the guidance they require. Thus, if the radar image itself is obsolete, what is no different today from the day when Riesman wrote about the "other-directed" type is that this type relies upon the vast array of signals—heard and seen—that vie for one's attention: "The other-directed person must be able to receive signals from far and near; the sources are many, the changes rapid."[15]

In *Faces in the Crowd*, the sequel to *The Lonely Crowd*, Riesman uses the radar metaphor to make the point that both types are conformists, but whereas the conformity of the "inner-directed" type rests "on the incorporation of adult authority," the conformity of the "other-directed" type rests on "sensitive attention to the expectations of contemporaries."[16] This, in turn, means that in contrast to the "inner-directed" person "who is steered toward lifelong goals" by the inner compass instilled at an early age, the "other-directed" person "obeys a fluctuating series of short-run goals" picked up by a radar that "is also installed in childhood, but the parents and other adults encourage the child to tune in to the people around him at any given time and share his preoccupation with their reactions to him and his to them."[17]

Riesman identifies a third type—"the tradition-directed person"—who didn't get much attention when *The Lonely Crowd* was receiving a lot of media attention. This is a person who lives in a society that is isolated from other societies and therefore changes very little over time. Culture controls each individual's behavior down to the minutest details. Well-developed rituals, routines, and religion provide clear orientation for everyone. Relationships to other members of the society are well defined. Some individuals are encouraged to develop a degree of individuality, but the range of personal choice is severely limited even for these persons. On the other hand, everyone belongs, for there are established roles even for those who deviate from the norm.[18] This type didn't get much attention because it was not the experience of the overwhelming majority of Americans. It illustrates, though, that the need for companionship becomes an issue with the other two types.

My use of John Bunyan's *The Pilgrim's Progress* to illustrate the "inner-directed" type suggests that this type is more likely than the "other-directed" type to have one or two lifelong companions with whom to share the journey of life, persons with whom they share common life goals. The "other-directed" type is more likely to have more companions and to relinquish earlier companions as they find that they are responding to different signals from the world around them. Riesman emphasizes that both types continue to exist in our society, and that this creates an inevitable "characterological struggle" in which the one rejects the values of the other.[19]

What I would like to emphasize, though, is that both types need and want companionship, for loneliness is a state we can endure only so long. I recall as a boy the time when my parents took us to a African Baptist Church to hear a performance of James Weldon Johnson's *God's Trombones*.[20] I especially remember "The Creation" poem, when a powerful male voice declared:

> And God stepped out on space,
> And he looked around and said:
> I'm lonely—
> I'll make me a world.

The voice continued, with the choir humming in the background, and described how God made the sun, the moon, and the stars, then looked at the hot and barren earth, and batted his eyes, and clapped his hands, raised his arm, and waved his hand, and the waters came, the grass began to grow, fishes and fowl, beasts and birds appeared, and God said: "That's good!" But he was still lonely, so he sat down on the side of a hill where he could think, until he thought: "I'll make me a man!" He scooped up clay from the river and kneeled down.

Now the voice became low and tender, but as the poem moved to its final climax, it steadily gained power, and the choir's voices reached a crescendo that sent shivers down my spine:

And there the great God Almighty
Who lit the sun and fixed it in the sky,
Who flung the stars to the most far corner of the
    night,
Who rounded the earth in the middle of his hand;
This Great God,
Like a mammy bending over her baby,
Kneeled down in the dust
Toiling over a lump of clay
Till he shaped it in his own image;
Then into it he blew the breath of life,
And man became a living soul.
Amen. Amen.

If God was lonely, and created the world to assuage his loneliness, then surely he did not intend us to be lonely. In fact, Genesis 2:18 tells us that after God took the man whom he had created and placed him in the garden of Eden, he said to himself, "It is not good that the man should be alone," and when it was evident that none of the animals or birds would be "fit" for him, God made a woman, or, as some would say, the man's "better half."

In the early 1970s, Henri J.M. Nouwen drew attention to the prevalence of loneliness in society in his book, *The Wounded Healer: Ministry in Contemporary Society.*[21] He wrote this book for the clergy, but reviewers who praised it for its clarity and simple profundity recommended it for laity as well. Anyone who seeks to be a Minister of Good Humor would find it to be an excellent companion to this book. In discussing how those who minister to others may make their own wounds a major source of their healing power, he asks, "But what are our wounds?"[22] How best to describe them? He answers: "Maybe the word 'loneliness' best expresses our immediate experience and therefore most fittingly enables us to understand our brokenness."[23] He continues: "We live in a society in which loneliness has become one of the most painful human wounds. The growing competition and rivalry which pervade our lives from birth have created in us an acute awareness of our isolation. This awareness has in turn left many with a heightened anxiety and an intense search for the experience of unity and community."[24] He suggests that the wound of loneliness in the life of the professional minister "hurts all the more, since he not only shares in the human condition of isolation, but also finds that his professional impact on others is diminishing"[25] Noting that many words have been used for the healing task of the Christian minister, he indicates that his choice is the word *hospitality* because it offers the best insight "into the nature of response to the human condition of loneliness."[26]

"A guy goes into a bar…" jokes would agree with the Bible that it is not good that anyone, man or woman, should be alone, and with Nouwen that loneliness has become one of the most painful human wounds. They depict solitary individuals entering the bar in search of community, but, above all, in search of true companionship, even if this companionship is of relatively short duration. Try to extend it to several hours, and the bartender will assuredly see to it that someone will take upon himself the unhappy task of dragging you out to his car and taking you home. (In one joke, a guy takes another guy home and makes the mistake of assuming that his tendency to slump on the ground is solely due to the fact that he is drunk; he learns otherwise when the guy's wife thanks him for bringing him home, then asks, "But where's his wheelchair?")

In "A guy goes into a bar…" jokes, some of the guys attempt to strike up a conversation with "a beautiful woman" (in the fictional world of the bar, the women are almost always described as "beautiful"). But these conversations with women usually lead eventually to a dead-end, or, at best, a cul-de-sac. I know of no jokes of this type in which the guy goes strolling out of the bar with the beautiful woman on his arm.

Rather, companionship is between two—possibly three—guys, and the jokes tend to play on some odd circumstance that brings the two—or three—together. Here's an example:

A guy goes into a bar to meet his old army buddy, and after spending a happy evening together, the two

G.I.s promise to meet again in ten years at the same bar, same time. Ten years later the first guy walks in, looks around, and sure enough, there is his old buddy on a barstool. He clasps his hand and cries, "The day we left I didn't think I'd really see you here!" The buddy looks up, stares, sways slightly, and asks, "Who left?"

In a society where so much is done by appointment, careful planning, checking and rechecking personal calendars to find a mutually convenient time to meet, companionship in the fictional bar happens by chance, and being unplanned, there is a greater likelihood that it will sweep away the pangs of loneliness.

Here's a joke where two guys meeting in a bar seems to take on a serendipitous quality, playing on the idea that a guy might meet another guy with whom he has so much in common that they will form, then and there, a lasting friendship:

A guy goes into a bar and stumbles up to the only other patron there and asks if he can buy him a drink. "Why, of course," comes the reply. The first man then asks, "Where are you from?' "I'm from Ireland," replies the second man. The first man responds, "You don't say, I'm from Ireland too! Let's have another round to Ireland." "Of course," replies the second man. Curious, the first man then asks, "Where in Ireland are you from?" "Dublin," comes the reply. "I can't believe it," says the first man, "I'm from Dublin too! Let's have another drink to Dublin." "Of course," replies the second man. Curiosity again strikes and the first man asks, "What school did you go to?" "Saint Mary's," replies the second man. "I graduated in 'sixty-two." "This is unbelievable," the first man says. "I went to Saint Mary's and I graduated in 'sixty-two!" At about that time in comes one of the regulars and sits down at the bar. "What's been going on?" he asks the bartender. "Nothing much," replies the bartender. "The O'Malley twins are drunk again."

I cannot speak for others, but the joke's setup, with the idea that two persons who grew up in the same neighborhood, or went to the same small college, or years earlier had a brief encounter in some far away country would unexpectedly meet again appeals to my sense of divine providence, that we are under the care of God's benevolent guidance. Stories of how two people who fell in love and spent the rest of their lives together happened to meet as if by chance but could easily have missed one another through some small circumstance—one of them deciding to take a different plane, the other deciding to leave a day earlier or later—I confess that I am an emotional pushover for these kinds of stories. I may, in fact, be even more impressed by these stories than the persons who actually lived them.

The joke about the O'Malley twins turns out not to be such a story, but when I first read it, I was drawn into the idea that two guys who had such similar personal histories would find one another in some local bar and begin a lasting friendship as a consequence of this chance meeting. When it turned out that there was a simple explanation for this seemingly fortuitous encounter, I had to admit to my disappointment, but, oddly enough, my disappointment made the joke seem all the funnier.

In any case, the joke illustrates our need and longing for companionship, and the way that new companionships are typically initiated. We rummage around in our personal histories for common experiences and perhaps give these common experiences a significance they would not have if we were merely reviewing our own personal story in isolation from the story of the other. The greater the ostensible difference between us, we cherish even more what we can claim in common, however fragile this may be. In his poem "Collecting Future Lives,"[27] Stephen Dunn relates how he and *his* brother would engage, in their twice-a-year visits, in the same "old repetitions" after their families had gone to bed. But if they allowed themselves to keep talking, and if they'd had enough to drink, they would get around to the fact that love was all that mattered, "the love they were cheated of / and the love they got, / the parental love / that if remembered at all / had been given, they decided, / and therefore could be given again." The guy who goes into the bar is seeking companionship, but he would not be unhappy if he also found some form or another of brotherly love.

The Need for Sympathy

Webster's New World College Dictionary has a number of definitions for *sympathy*. The most relevant are "an entering into, or the ability to enter into, another person's mental state, feelings, emotions, etc.," and "pity or compassion felt for another's troubles."[28] It's something of a cliché that a guy goes into the bar to assuage his need for sympathy. His marriage is in disarray, he's going nowhere at work, he feels lousy, and no one seems to care if he lives or dies. He isn't looking for therapy, and probably has little respect for those who do, but he wouldn't mind at all if someone were to ask him how he's doing, or expressed a little sympathy for him. In most social settings, people are preoccupied with their own troubles, and don't have the time or inclination to see that someone else is hurting. But, in his poem "Scars," William Stafford, who undoubtedly has his own problems, notices a woman in church who has known pain, and then his eyes turn to the children who, one day, will know it too:

> They tell how it was, and how time
> came along, and how it happened
> again and again. They tell
> the slant life takes when it turns
> and slashes your face as a friend.
> Any wound is real. In church
> a woman lets the sun find
> her cheek, and we see the lesson:
> there are years in that book; there are sorrows
> a choir can't reach when they sing.
> Rows of children lift their faces of promise,
> Places where the scars will be. [29]

"A guy goes into a bar..." jokes that address the need for sympathy divide rather neatly into three types: the ones in which a guy, sitting all by himself, looks so utterly forlorn that someone takes pity on him and goes to his table and sits down to try to cheer him up; the ones where a guy pours out his troubles to the bartender; and the ones where a guy deserves sympathy but he is either too proud to seek it or too stupid to know that he deserves it. Here's an example of the first type:

> A guy goes into a bar, orders a drink, and stares at it for a half hour without moving. A big truck driver finally walks up to him, takes the guy's drink and guzzles it down in one swig. The poor man starts crying. The truck driver says, "Come on, man, I was just joking. Here, I'll buy you another drink. I can't stand seeing a man cry." "No, it's not that," says the man. "This day is the worst of my life. First, I fall asleep and get to the office late. My boss is outraged, and he fires me. When I leave the building to go to my car, I find out it was stolen. I get a cab to return home, and when I get out I remember I left my wallet and credit cards in my car. I enter my house and I find my wife in bed with the gardener. I leave home and come to this bar. And while I'm thinking about putting an end to my life, you show up and drink my poison…"

In this joke, there's a joke within a joke. The guy who comes over doesn't say flat out, "Hey, buddy, what's the trouble?" Instead, he tries to lighten the other man up with a humorous touch. But the guy is too far gone to respond to the gesture. When the good Samaritan thinks the guy starts crying because he grabbed his drink, the guy assures him that this isn't what's making him cry—well, at least, that's not the whole story. Then he pours it all out: he's been fired, his car has been stolen, he caught his wife in bed with the gardener, and, to top it all off, some stranger comes over and drinks his poison. To anyone else, the stranger's act would have been a godsend, an act of divine grace—but not this guy. He's so low that the stranger's action was the straw that broke the camel's back.

It's probably a minor point, but it's easy to overlook that his day got off to a bad start when he slept in and was late for work. In *Reality Therapy*, William Glasser writes about the importance of responsibility. He emphasizes that the therapist should never condone the irresponsible behavior of the client in the real world, nor should the therapist ever imply "that what he [the therapist] does, what he [himself] stands for, or what he [himself] values is unimportant."[30] The therapist, he adds, has to be "tough, interested, human, and sensitive."[31] I wholeheartedly agree. This is a vital prescription for good therapy. But, unless it was proven that the man in the joke had a history of tardiness, it would seem that he was justified in feeling that his boss overreacted. (Who hasn't had a boss who had a gift for overreacting?) And who can doubt that he was the victim of bad luck when his car was stolen? His wife's affair with the gardener, who has taken the place of the milkman as a threat to domestic harmony, may have been her way of letting him know that he is a lousy husband and inadequate lover. Still, you have to feel for a guy who comes home in the middle of the day because he got fired at work and discovers his wife in bed with another guy, especially a guy he is paying to keep the outside premises looking nice. So it probably wouldn't do for another guy—even a big and presumably tough truck driver—to point out to him that he shouldn't have slept in, much less suggest that, in doing so, he brought all of his troubles on himself. No, we have all experienced days when everything seems to go wrong, and anyone who has had one of those days deserves our heartfelt, uncompromising sympathy.

Another example of the first type of joke, where a guy goes over and sits down with a guy who is down in the dumps, is this one:

> A guy goes into a bar and sees a friend at a table drinking by himself. Approaching the friend he comments, "You look terrible, what's the problem?" "My mother died in June," he says, "and left me $10,000." "Gee, that's tough," he replies. "Then in July," the friend continues, "my father died, leaving me $50,000." "Wow, two parents gone in two months, no wonder you're depressed." "And last month, my

aunt died and left me $15,000." "Three close family members lost in three months? How sad." "Then, this month," continues the friend, "nothing!"

As any person with an ounce of feeling would do, the friend picks up on the deaths that the poor guy has suffered, in comparison with which the monetary gains are insignificant.

Not so the guy who has elicited this friend's sympathy. The guy has been on a remarkable roll (in his eyes), and when it ends, his self-pity knows no bounds. Lurking behind this joke are the myriad family tales of the surviving members of a family squabbling over the money that the deceased left behind—a distraction, perhaps, from their genuine sense of grief and loss, but unseemly just the same. This joke, though, illustrates my point that "A guy goes into a bar…" jokes assume that anyone who looks the least bit down deserves a sympathetic response and that someone should make a point of offering it.

The second type of joke that illustrates the need for sympathy is the one in which a patron pours out his troubles to the bartender. That lending a sympathetic ear is integral to the bartender's role is a fundamental tenet of "A guy goes into a bar…" jokes. Marital problems top the list of troubles in this particular type. Here's an example:

A guy goes into a bar and orders a triple Scotch whiskey. The bartender pours him the drink and says, "That's quite a heavy drink. What's wrong?" After downing his drink, the guy says, "I got home and found my wife in bed with my best friend." "Wow," says the bartender. "No wonder you needed a stiff drink. The second triple is on the house." As the man downs his second triple Scotch, the bartender asks him, "What did you do?" The guys says, "I walked over to my wife, looked her straight in the eye, and told her that we were through and to pack up and leave." The bartender says, "That makes sense, but what about your best friend?" The guy says, "I walked over to him, looked him right in the eye, and said, 'Bad dog!'"

No doubt, this particular joke is as "bad" as the dog in the joke. But it plays on the "a dog is a man's best friend" cliché and also parodies the recommended method for housebreaking a dog ("bad dog"). For our purposes here, however, the central point is that the bartender initiated the conversation by asking the man, "What's wrong?" He didn't wait for the man to begin his tale of woe.

Here's a joke in which the guy tells the bartender what recently happened between his wife and himself and tries to put the best face on it:

> A guy goes into a bar. "Pour me a stiff one, Eddie. I just had another fight with the little woman," "Oh, yeah?" says Eddie. "And how did this one end?" "When it was over," the guy replies, "she came to me on her hands and knees." "Really? Now that's a switch! What did she say?" "She said, 'Come out from under the bed, you gutless weasel!'"

Being called a "weasel" is not very complimentary. As *Webster's New World College Dictionary* points out, *weasel* has the implication of avoiding or evading a commitment or responsibility, and "*weasel* words," probably based on the weasel's habit of sucking out the contents of an egg without destroying the shell, implies "words or remarks that are equivocal or deliberately ambiguous or misleading."[32] The story the guy tells the bartender is, in fact, an illustration of his tendency to use weasel words, thus unintentionally supporting his wife's allegation. Even so, we don't expect that the bartender will suggest that the guy take a good look at himself in the mirror to see if his wife has a point. To do so would violate the fundamental assumptions of sympathetic listening.

Finally, here's a joke that suggests that even a long-suffering bartender has his limits, but only because the subject is not one of the usual ones of marital strife, problems at work, etc.

> A guy goes into a bar and approaches the bartender, saying, "I've been working on a top secret project on

molecular genetics for the past five years and I've just got to talk to someone about it." The bartender says, "Wait a minute. Before we talk about that, just answer a few questions. When a deer defecates, why does it come out like little pellets?" The guy doesn't know. The bartender then asks, "Why is it that when a dog poops, it lands on the ground and looks like a coiled rope?" The guy, again, says, "I don't have any idea." The bartender then says, "You don't know crap and you want to talk about molecular genetics?"

I don't know about you, but in this case, my own sympathies are with the bartender. I think that this hotshot biologist deserved what he got.

The third type of the need for sympathy joke is one where the guy is too proud to ask for it or too dumb to know that he deserves it. Here's an example of being too proud:

A cowboy goes into a bar after riding his horse into a new town. Unfortunately, the locals have a habit of picking on strangers. When he finishes his drink, he finds that his horse has been stolen. He goes back into the bar, handily flips his gun in the air, catches it above his head without even looking, and fires a shot into the ceiling. "Which one of you sidewinders stole my hoss?" he yells with surprising forcefulness. No one answers. "All right, I'm gonna have another beer, and if my hoss ain't back outside by the time I finish, I'm gonna do what I done in Texas! And I don't want to have to do what I done in Texas!" He has another beer, walks outside, and his horse is back! He saddles up and starts to ride out of town. The bartender wanders out of the bar and asks, "Say, partner, before you go…What did you do in Texas?" The cowboy turns back and sighs, "I had to walk home."

Because the cowboy is a stranger in a town that has a habit of picking on strangers, we can certainly appreciate why he didn't walk into the bar, order a beer, and say to the bartender, "I'm really feeling down. My horse just got stolen, and he means the world to me. Me and him have been partners for a good many years. Without my horse, I'm nothing." Instead, he came in, flashed his gun, and threatened the patrons with violence—or so they thought. Proud men—and women—tend to think that the need for sympathy is beneath them, that it's a sign of weakness. So they go it alone.

Then there are those who are too dumb to realize that they deserve sympathy:

> Bill and Fred, both construction workers, were having a beer after work. Bill said, "Hey, Fred, I've been noticing that the foreman's been knocking off work an hour early. I've got a great idea. Since he knocks off early, let's you and me knock off early too." So they agreed to try it. The next evening they were back in the bar having a beer. Fred said to Bill, "Hey, knocking off an hour early today was great. Let's do it again tomorrow." Bill replied, "Nope, too risky. As soon as I got home yesterday afternoon, I looked all over for my wife. Finally, I opened the bedroom door, and there she was in bed with the foreman. I quietly closed the door and tiptoed out of the house and came down here. I almost got caught!"

This joke obviously plays off the fear of getting caught in bed with another man's wife, a much greater crime than taking off work an hour early. But it also illustrates how someone may deserve sympathy but is unaware of it. There could be any number of reasons for this unawareness: The belief that one has brought the calamity upon oneself, the belief that only those who are perfect are worthy of sympathy, or the belief that others are much more deserving of sympathy.

Implications for Good Humor Ministry

If this book had been written back in the 1960s, readers would have expected that I would wrap this chapter up by extolling the virtues of bar ministry: ministry carried out by clergypersons, wearing ordinary garb, in local taverns—one of various ways in which the churches were seeking to bring the gospel to persons who "would not be caught dead in a church." This chapter is on an entirely different—in fact, the opposite—trajectory. I believe that "A guy goes into a bar..." jokes have a great deal to teach us about fundamental human needs, and how we might go about meeting them more often than we do. As I have proposed, these jokes lift up the need for attention, for companionship, and for sympathy. They also tell us a great deal about how these needs may be responded to.

The Need for Attention

For the need for attention, we should recognize that this need probably goes back to childhood, and to the fact that all of us suffered attention deficits at that time that will probably take a whole lifetime to make up for. Since this need goes so far back, we should be careful not to be critical of someone who appears to be an "attention-getter," or persons who talk too much in a meeting, sing too loudly in church, or brag too much about their achievements or about the giftedness of their kids. Instead, think of them as trying to make up for earlier attention deficits—those times when they yearned for recognition by their parents, their teachers, the popular kids in class. Think of them, too, as using these attention-getting methods to achieve a feeling of belonging—and think, too, that when they have a secure sense that they belong, they may not have to talk so much, sing so loudly, or brag so much. When this happens, they may be outstanding recruits in the Ministry of Good Humor.

As for those who came to church and did not come back because "no one paid any attention" to them, I remember that when I was a kid there was one man who hung around the narthex and made a point of greeting everyone, but especially strangers, with a handshake and a friendly hello. Maybe the fact that I remember this man so many years later is because he was such a rare bird. For the rest of us, the following case might be instructive. I wrote about it in my book *Reframing*.[33] There's a method used in psychotherapy called "paradoxical intention." It involves instructing clients to wish to bring about the very thing they fear will happen. When they wish for it to happen, they discover that it does not happen because the wishing and the fearing are two opposites that cancel each other out. Take the case of a woman who couldn't walk down a street where there were other people on the sidewalk because she feared she would push one in front of an approaching car or bus. One morning her therapist accompanied her out on the street, and when a car approached, the therapist said to the woman, "Now, push me in front of the car." The client couldn't do it. This method has been used quite successfully with persons with phobias. It occurred to me that it might be used in churches where the regular members have a "phobia" relating to the greeting of strangers. In *Reframing*, I imagined the following scenario:

At an elders' meeting, there was general consensus that the congregation was unfriendly to visitors. They agreed that they needed to be friendlier, and admitted to feeling guilty for not talking to new visitors or sporadic attendees as much as they should. The minister said that he had heard such discussions many times before and knew they rarely had much effect. So he made the following radical request: "For the next few Sundays between now and our next elders' meeting, I want you to go out of your way to *avoid* our visitors or anyone else who comes in alone. If you find yourself tempted to greet one of them, restrain yourself. And if one of them happens to approach you, I want you to turn away and talk, instead, to a friend. Then, at our next elders meeting, I'll ask each of you to report on how successful you were in avoiding them."

When someone asked why he would want the elders to behave in such a rude way, the minister explained that he could handle the task of greeting visitors and solitary people himself and that most of them want to maintain their anonymity anyway. He added that the elders had their own problems trying to keep their own kids in some semblance of order, or getting some essential church work done in the precious time available. These were arguments that he had actually heard voiced by some parishioners. These arguments provided a plausible rationale for his reasoning.

Some elders remained puzzled about his request, some felt it was a trick, but all agreed to follow his instructions.

At the next elders' meeting, there was a discussion of their "success" in avoiding visitors and solitary individuals. Not all had violated the minister's instructions, but many had. Overall, however, they had a very different discussion from the one that would have taken place if the elders had been asked to report on their efforts to make contact with visitors and solitary persons. The conversation was much more alive and spirited, and there was none of the negative self-recrimination which had characterized their earlier discussions of the issue.[34]

To remain perfectly faithful to the method of paradoxical intention, I am certainly not advocating for this application of it. I think it's a dumb idea. I trust that you do too. If so, there's an alternative approach: As "A guy goes into a bar…" jokes suggest, most of us are more comfortable with the attention we receive from others if it focuses less on ourselves and more on something we have with us. Few of us go around with a singing frog on the shoulder or a piano-playing hamster in a coat pocket. But there's usually something about us that merits a friendly comment: "Your baby is so cute, and he looks just like you!" Or, "What a lovely handbag. You have wonderful taste!" Trivial? Empty chatter? I don't think so. And anyway, the Ministry of Good Humor isn't about probing the depths of one another's psyche or soul. It's perfectly content to remain on the surface of things. But surfaces are not necessarily superficial, and no one knows this better than the patron of the fictional bar where everyone gets at least a little attention, which is more than can be said for a lot of other places in this rather inhospitable world of ours.

The Need for Companionship

As for what "A guy goes into a bar…" jokes teach us about the need for companionship, I would want to emphasize, first, that the best way to address this need is to keep the scheduling part of it to a bare minimum. Here's an example: I meet for lunch with a friend from our seminary days who has lived for a couple of decades in the general vicinity of Princeton, but I didn't know it until he found out that I teach at Princeton Theological Seminary and he knocked on my office door one day, wondering if I was up for lunch that day. He drives us to where we have lunch and drives me back. As I begin to exit the car on a busy Princeton street, I say, "How about three weeks from today? October 23?" and he either says, "You're on," or "Wednesday that week works better for me," and I say, "Works for me, too. See you then." Out I get, and off he goes. I say, keep companionship simple. Don't load it with more burdens than it can handle. As Jesus said, "My yoke is easy, and my burden is light" (Mt. 11:30).

My second point is that companionship is fostered through recognition of experiences shared in common. The friend I met for lunch and I discovered early on that we have sons, and that we care about what happens to them. We also discovered some differences. I prefer Jesus to Paul, while for my friend, Paul is the greater of the two because he put Christianity on the map. I've learned greater appreciation for Paul from this friend. And he's now talking about what a brilliant guy Jesus was, that his sayings are the best thing going.

The Need for Sympathy

What "A guy goes into a bar..." jokes teach us is that sympathy is likely to be biased in favor of the person who is sitting next to or across from us. I often hear from students that "A guy goes into a bar..." jokes are misogynist because they put wives down, and sexist because they treat the women who dare to enter this fictional bar as sex objects. I won't attempt to challenge these contentions. But the point that I consider worth making is that the wife jokes are less about wives and more about the human need for sympathy, and sympathy, I would argue, does not entail making a case for the wife who isn't there. We should assume, rather, that she has her own friends who commiserate with her about the jackass that she married, most likely 'til death do them part.

We also learn from these jokes that there are essentially three ways in which the need for sympathy might be addressed. One is when a sympathetic soul notices that someone else appears troubled or discouraged, and takes the initiative to ask if this is so. Another is when the person who needs sympathy approaches the one whose profession it is to offer sympathy and, in effect, solicits it, either directly or indirectly. The indirect approach in this context is to order "a stiff drink" and leave it to the professional to identify the cue. The direct approach is to order the stiff drink and explain why. Since the indirect approach is probably the most common, the professional is expected to be able to pick up the cue and, in effect, ask the troubled person if he wants to talk about it. The third way that the need for sympathy may be addressed is to recognize that this need lurks behind some false bravado or inability even to recognize that one's situation merits the sympathy of others.

I think it is important to point out that, in two of the ways, no professional is involved. This two-to-one ratio would seem to be a good one for a congregation to aspire to. It is also useful to note that the professional exercised the right to reject the request of the man who wanted to talk about a topic which was obviously beyond the professional's competence. His manner of demurring may not have been entirely straightforward, but that would seem to be beside the point. Conversely, the fact that he was available to talk about marital issues was taken for granted. Moreover, the person's preference for one over the other of these ways of expressing one's need for sympathy was treated with respect.

Another point deserves mention in a book designed to encourage its readers to enlist in the corps of Ministers of Good Humor. In one of the jokes I used to illustrate the need for sympathy—the one about the truck driver who went over to the table of the guy who was staring at his drink—there was an overt use of humor. The truck driver grabbed the guy's drink and swigged it down. When the guy began to cry, the truck driver explained that he "was only joking." It seems useful to point out that the joke misfired, and that the truck driver was the victim of his own attempt to be funny. You will recall my citation, in the first chapter, of Proverbs 26:18–19: "Like a maniac who shoots deadly firebrands and arrows, / so is one who deceives a neighbor / and says, 'I am only joking!'" The two situations are very different, but both illustrate the hazards of "only joking."

Thus, despite appearances, the intent of this chapter has not been to encourage Ministers of Good Humor to tell jokes and do funny things. Instead, it has been to encourage them to attempt to create an ethos akin to the one evident in the bar, where fundamental human needs for attention, companionship, and sympathy are attended to. Take a lesson from the guy who runs the joint: the bartender may occasionally crack a joke, but his job is to create an atmosphere of mutual respect and decorum within which others are enabled to express these needs. When a guy goes into a bar, his thirst is likely to be assuaged. But this could happen anywhere. What the bar offers is an ethos in which one is the object of an attentive eye, an extended hand, a sympathethic ear. We can learn important lessons from what transpires in this place that is no place, but could be any place.

3

Good Humor Role Models

Lawyers, Parrots, and Blondes

Sigmund Freud was born in the small Moravian town of Freiburg, with 4,500 inhabitants, in 1856. His father, Jakob, was a poor wool merchant who had been married twice before he married Freud's mother, Amalia, who was twenty years younger. Freud's father's two sons from a previous marriage lived nearby. Freud, born above the blacksmith shop where his parents rented rooms, was Jakob and Amalia's first child, but many siblings were to join him in quick succession. By the time the family settled in Vienna four years after Freud was born, there were two additional children, a sister Anna and a brother Julius, but Julius died at the age of seven months. Over the next six years, five more children—four girls (Rose, Marie, Adolfine, and Pauline) and one son (Alexander)—brought the total number of children to seven. His father had a difficult time supporting this large of a family. He was likable, generous, and told amusing stories, but he was unable to cope with the industrializing world around him. As time went on, he relied on the resources of his older sons from previous marriages, who had moved to England and were doing well there.

Freud was able to attend the University of Vienna, beginning medical studies while living at home, but was always strapped for funds. When he became a resident at General Hospital in Vienna, he was able to move from his family home to the hospital, but his salary, 30 florin per month, was barely sufficient to live on. His father was unable to support the family, so Freud tried to contribute a minimum of 10 florin each month to help out his parents, younger sisters, and brother. Some months, he simply couldn't manage to live on 20 florin, so he reluctantly turned to borrowing. An old Hebrew teacher named Samuel Hammerschlag, two colleagues at the Physiological Institute, and a local physician, Josef Breuer, would give him money.

Freud got engaged at this time, and he wrote a letter to his fiancée, Martha Bernays, about the monetary gifts that he was receiving from others. Samuel Hammerschlag, who was quite elderly, had invited Freud to his home and after telling Freud about his own poverty as a young man, he gave Freud fifty florin. Freud told Martha that the old man had given him money, unsolicited, in the past. He added that he had felt ashamed at first, but that when the old man made it clear that he did not expect repayment and did not want Freud to feel obligated in any way, he "accepted the idea of being indebted to good men and those of our faith without the feeling of personal obligation."[1] Continuing his account of this evening's visit, Freud told Martha that when his old teacher gave him the money, he told him he would spend it on his family. His benefactor objected: "He was very much against this idea, saying that I worked very hard and could not at the moment afford to help other people." Freud added, "But I did make it clear to him that I must spend at least half the money in this way."[2]

Why am I telling this story? What do Freud's money worries and his acceptance of a gift from his old Hebrew teacher have to do with the Ministry of Good Humor? The short answer is simple: *accepting a gift produced strong and mixed feelings in Freud.* The long answer requires that we probe a little further into Freud's personal circumstances at the time. I guarantee that there will be a valuable payoff from this biographical excursion for our understanding of the Ministry of Good Humor.

In his book *The Jokes of Sigmund Freud*, Elliott Oring notes that "the gifts and loans that he received from his benefactors generated in Freud feelings of indebtedness, dependence, and resentment," and suggests that "these feelings continued throughout his life, despite the subsequent improvements in his economic situation."[3] The very fact that these feelings continued throughout his life, even when he was not relying on the generosity of others, indicates that the situation of being placed in a position where he was accepting handouts was emotionally difficult for him.

Evenings like the one he had just endured were painful. Despite whatever gratitude he may have felt, accepting these gifts was personally demeaning. He knew that he could not treat these gifts as loans, which he would soon repay. He knew that he had no prospect of an inheritance or huge increase in salary. While other sons of impoverished fathers may have been able to count on a rich uncle, thereby at least keeping the situation within the family, his uncle Josef, his father's brother, had been indicted, convicted, and imprisoned for trading in counterfeit rubles. His own father and half-brothers may have been implicated in his uncle's schemes.[4] He wasn't even sure he could afford to get married, much less repay the men who had taken pity on him and volunteered to help him. In fact, he and Martha had become engaged only two months after they first met, and both knew full well that this "was not a prudent move."[5] She came from a family of some prominence, but her father had left her mother with little money when he died, and she had no money of her own. Her mother didn't think Freud was suitable for her daughter, but, being without means herself, she couldn't keep Martha from marrying him if this was what she was determined to do. They were engaged for five years, though, before he felt he was professionally secure enough to marry. During their engagement, they remained in contact largely through letters, because he could not afford frequent visits to her home in Wandsbek, Germany.

We can imagine that each time he accepted a gift from a well-to-do benefactor, Freud thought about his father, and felt ashamed to be the son of Jakob Freud, a man who was unable to support his own family, and who depended heavily on his two older sons and his much younger son, who was himself struggling to get established in life, for their support. We can also imagine that Freud would feel much better about taking the money if he could inform his benefactor that he would not be keeping it for himself, but would be giving it to his family. Even so, it must have been an awkward moment when, after receiving the gift, he and his benefactor would get involved in a discussion of how he would spend it. I can imagine his benefactor wondering at this point whether he should have given the money to Freud at all—"I meant it for Sigmund, the boy who was my student some years ago"—and I can also imagine Freud saying to himself, "The problem with taking gifts from anyone is that they instruct you on how to spend it."

So, how did Freud deal with these feelings of his? Surprisingly, he turned to jokes. No doubt, when he was growing up, joke-telling adults or other boys introduced him to beggar (called "the *schnorrer*") jokes and marriage broker (called "the *schadchen*") jokes. But both of these joke types assumed greater significance for him as he thought about the gifts he had received and his extended engagement to Martha. Both were difficult, and these jokes helped to relieve the emotional distress. He began collecting a large file of jokes and eventually wrote a book on the subject of jokes. His first and best-known book, *The Interpretation of Dreams*,[6] was published in 1900. The next year, his book *The Psychopathology of Everyday Life: Forgetting, Slips of the Tongue, Bungled Actions, Superstitions, and Errors*[7] appeared. Four years later, *Jokes and Their Relation to the Unconscious*[8] was published. The first two books proved to be enormously successful. The book on jokes fell as flat as an off-color joke told to a group of uptight Presbyterians. His Jewish friends were especially indignant that he had made their jokes available to outsiders. They felt that non-Jews would view the jokes as confirming their negative stereotypes of Jews. In his autobiography, published twenty years later, he referred to his book on jokes as a "side-issue" to his book on dreams.[9] So even he tended to discount it.

I have no intention of providing a summary of a 300-page book, even a book whose subject matter is jokes. Instead, I'll skip over the preceding pages and head straight for the very last paragraph. Here, Freud states his theory about why we like jokes and other types of humor. The reason, he says, is that humor *saves in the expenditure of painful emotions, costly inhibitions, and difficult thinking.*[10]

Why would we want to save ourselves from these three inner experiences or processes? Freud provides an explanation later, in his 1915 article, "Thoughts for the Times on War and Death."[11] In this article, he says that the price we pay for living in civilized society is that we live, *psychologically speaking, beyond our means.*[12] Put another way, psychologically we are spending our future earnings today. In terms of the benefits we talked about in chapter one, the fact that we are psychologically overextended accounts for the fact that we are anxious, stressed out, and subject to depression. Our credit is greatly overdrawn.

In his only other work on humor, a brief article titled "Humor,"[13] published twenty-three years later, Freud referred to this as his "economic" view of humor. In this article, it was clear that he was most interested in the saving in the expenditure of painful emotions. Now, I think that we can readily understand the saving of painful emotions and difficult thinking, but the idea of saving costly inhibitions may seem a little strange, for how do you "save" on something that you are inhibited from doing? Freud's point is that it takes psychological resources to inhibit oneself from saying or doing something you would dearly love to say or do, but you know that if you said or did it, others would disapprove. So, it takes more psychological energy to *keep* from saying or doing it than it would take to go ahead and say it or do it.[14]

Freud was especially interested in the uses of humor in general, and jokes in particular, to save the expenditure of painful emotions. He cites the joke about a convicted criminal who is being led to the gallows in the wintertime. As they move toward the hangman's noose, he asks the guards to go fetch him a scarf so that he won't catch a cold. In this joke, and others like it, "a man adopts a humorous attitude toward himself in order to ward off possible suffering."[15]

Jokes about Beggars

But back to Freud and his interest in jokes about beggars and marriage brokers, beginning with the beggars. In his letter to Martha about his meeting with his old Hebrew teacher, Freud wrote that he "accepted the idea of being indebted to good men and those of our faith without the feeling of personal obligation." This statement suggests that he would ordinarily have "the feeling of personal obligation," but he doesn't really want to have it. In terms of his economic theory of humor formulated a decade or so later, he wanted to save in the expenditure of the feeling of personal obligation. In other words, he didn't want to *feel* personal obligation. That he was personally obligated to these "good men," men of "our faith," was pretty hard to deny on objective grounds, but it was actually they (especially his benefactor Josef Breuer) who told him he should not feel personally obligated. It was a gift, pure and simple.

Beggar jokes helped him *not* to have this feeling of personal obligation. There are four beggar jokes in his book on jokes. In three of them, the beggar acts as though he has a right to what the rich man gives him because the rich man owes it to him. Why? Because it is the sacred duty of a rich man to give to a poor man when the poor man asks for charity. In fact, by asking for charity, the poor man does the rich man a service, as this enables the rich man to fulfill his sacred duty. As Theodor Reik points out in his book on *Jewish Wit*:

> It has often been said that the Jewish giver does not bestow benefits on the poor in giving him money, and his actions do not deserve the name of goodness or kindness. He simply fulfills his religious duty, and the beneficiary need not, in the strict sense of the word, be grateful to him. On the contrary, the donor owes some gratitude to the receiver because the beneficiary gave him the opportunity to attain high religious merit.[16]

By referring to his benefactors as men "of our faith," Freud was suggesting that they were performing their religious duty when they gave money to this young, struggling medical student.

In the first of these beggar jokes, a beggar approaches a wealthy baron with the request for some money for his trip to Ostend, a seaport in northwest Belgium on the North Sea. His doctors, he explained, had recommended sea-bathing to restore his health. The rich man said that he would give him something, but did he have to go to Ostend, the most expensive of all sea-bathing resorts? The beggar replied indignantly, "Sir, I consider nothing too expensive for my health!"[17] Freud comments that the beggar's response is technically correct, for what could be more valuable to the man than his health? But the beggar acts as though it was his *own* money that he was to prepared to sacrifice for his health, as though the money and the health were the concern of the same person.[18]

In the second beggar joke, a beggar who was a regular guest at the same house every Sunday appeared one day in the company of an unknown young man who gave signs that he was about to sit down at the table. "Who is this?" the householder asked. The beggar replied, "He's been my son-in-law since last week. I promised him his board for the first year."[19] Freud points out that the beggar treats the wealthy man's food as if it belongs to him. He adds that the "sacred ordinances of the Jews" almost give him "a right to make this confusion."[20] This joke comes especially close to the scene in Samuel Hammerschlag's home when Freud virtually claimed the right to give his family the money that the old man had just given him. But where the actual experience caused him to have all sorts of mixed feelings, none of them positive, the beggar in the joke exhibits no confusion of feeling whatsoever. The householder had made an offer to him, and he had, in turn, made an offer to his son-in-law. One can almost imagine him saying to the householder, "You have a problem with that?"

In the third beggar joke, a beggar tells another beggar not to bother to ask the rich man for money today because he's in a bad mood and has been giving no one more than one measly florin. The other beggar replies that he is going to beg just the same, for, "Why should I give *him* a florin? Does he give *me* anything?"[21] Freud notes that this joke seems utterly nonsensical unless one takes into consideration the rich man's obligation to give to the poor. Thus, in a sense, the florin belongs to the beggar, so why shouldn't he go and collect what is his? If he doesn't, he will be giving the rich man a florin, and why should *he* give the man something when, technically, the man hasn't given him anything?

The fourth beggar joke takes the rich man's point of view. This is the story of the Baron who is so deeply moved by a beggar's tale of woe that he rings for his servants, saying, "Throw him out! He's breaking my heart!"[22] Freud notes that the viewpoint of this joke is in "open rebellion" against the religious viewpoint that it is the sacred duty of the rich to give to the poor. In effect, it expresses the complaint that there isn't any advantage in being a rich man if you are a Jew because "other people's misery makes it impossible to enjoy one's own happiness."[23] Theodor Reik relates a joke in which even the pretense of compassion for the beggar is absent: "A beggar complains to a rich man that he hasn't eaten for three days. The rich man responds: 'Sometimes one has to force oneself.'"[24]

If we look at the internal dynamics of these jokes, as Freud proposes, it doesn't require a Ph.D. in clinical psychology to see that the jokes overcome *costly inhibition*. It's pretty obvious that there was a lot of bad feeling about the sacred duty of charity in the Austrian Jewish community and this goes equally for the poor who needed assistance from the wealthy, and the wealthy who felt obligated to help them. The jokes say what the community is not supposed to say—they overcome the inhibition that would normally prevail—but they do so in such a way that both the teller of the joke and the hearer of the joke experience pleasure.

Freud thinks that there is an additional factor in these particular jokes: the emergence of the middle class.[25] They are neither filthy rich nor desperately poor. They are struggling too, and do not expect the rich to bail them out if they get into a jam, so what is their obligation to those who are poorer than they? He suggests that an "ordinary, middle-class view of charity" has developed over time, and it conflicts with the "sacred duty" viewpoint. He means, I believe, that the middle-class view is that giving to those worse off than oneself is a strictly voluntary act of benevolence, and, if this is so, the receiver of the gift *should* be grateful, and should *not* act as though he or she is enabling the donor to carry out his or her sacred obligation. Thus, the middle-class, as the very term implies, are caught in the middle, and these jokes about the beggar and the very rich enable them to say, indirectly, what they are not supposed to say: that they resent the absence of gratitude when they give to the poor.

Once when I was sitting in the dentist's chair for a root canal, the dentist and her assistant were listening to a local talk show. The subject was making donations to the poor and needy. Considerable debate was generated by a caller's account of how she had organized a project to provide needy individuals and families with a nourishing Thanksgiving dinner plus cans of food and so on. In exchange, she asked that the recipients write a brief note of thanks, presumably so that she could use these comments to inspire other donors to participate in the project the following year. Because no thank-you notes were received, she said that she felt the recipients did not exhibit the appropriate gratitude and therefore she would not organize the project the following year. As my dentist and her assistant came down on opposite sides of the question of whether she was justified in feeling the way she did, I wanted to chime in and cite the story of the ten lepers in Luke 17:11–19 and to express my opinion that if the woman had received even *one* thank-you note, she would have decided to repeat the project a second year. Unable to join in the conversation (my mouth being otherwise occupied), I did the next best thing afterward, which was to thank the dentist and assistant for a conversation between them that distracted me from the root canal procedure itself. This brings me to a second point about beggar jokes.

Through the telling or hearing of these jokes, an individual who has been involved in the situations they portray may experience relief of the *painful emotions* the situations originally evoked. In his article on "Humor," Freud suggests that jokes are like telling a child who is frightened by thunder, "There's nothing to fear. Think of it as something to laugh about!"[26] In my day, the idea was that the Seven Dwarfs had decided to go bowling. But whatever the alternative "think about..." might be, the painful emotion of fear would vanish. In much the same way, these beggar jokes would have enabled Freud himself to gain an emotional detachment from the experience of being a recipient of the gifts of his benefactors, from the "feelings of indebtedness, dependence, and resentment."[27] We can well imagine that these jokes enabled him to look back on the scenes that he describes in his letter to Martha and to view them with much less emotional intensity than he had experienced at the time. Those memories might still produce a rueful wince or two, but the strong feelings of indebtedness, dependence, and resentment would fade, and only the pleasure of the joke itself would remain. This may seem a rather strange basis on which to make a case for humor, for it implies that the great value of humor is in what it *doesn't* evoke in us. But for persons who are emotionally overextended, this can be a blessing, nearly as liberating as being told that your sins are forgiven, that all the old debts have been paid off, and you no longer have a mortgaged future.

Jokes about Marriage Brokers

In his book on jokes, Freud has seven jokes about marriage brokers. In his social context, marriage brokers were respected about as much as the proverbial used-car salesman would be in ours. Marriage brokers were considered a necessary evil. They were expected to have intimate knowledge of the history of the families in the community because they served as protection against the inadvertent union of blood relatives. So they were viewed as snoops and rumormongers. More broadly, they were "brokers." Their official job was to serve, for a fee, of course, as the agent for parents who hoped to marry off their daughter to a man whose social and economic position would be advantageous. The daughter's desires were of little or no account. Since there was no marriage broker involved in Freud's engagement to Martha Bernays, his case was different. But his lengthy engagement to Martha, and the doubts that her mother had expressed concerning his suitability, meant that the marriage broker jokes could serve in this case much the same purpose that the beggar jokes served in relation to his financial difficulties. They could assist him in gaining emotional distance or detachment from the feelings that his long and difficult engagement had evoked in him.

Freud notes that in the marriage broker jokes, the broker resorts to faulty reasoning or out-and-out sophistry to persuade the young man to marry the daughter of the parents who had engaged him. Here's a typical one:[28]

> The marriage broker was defending the girl he had proposed against the young man's protests. The young man points out, "I don't care much for the girl's mother. She's a disagreeable, stupid person." The broker replies, "But after all, you're not marrying the mother. What you want is her daughter." "Yes, but she's no longer young, and she's hardly a beauty." "No matter. If she's neither young nor beautiful she'll be all the more faithful to you." "She hasn't much money." "Who's talking about money? Are you marrying money? It's a wife that you want." "But she's got a hunchback too." "Well, what *do* you want? She's not to have a single fault?"

Freud points out that in this joke there is "the appearance of logic which is characteristic of a piece of sophistry and which is intended to conceal the faulty reasoning."[29] The broker, he adds, acts as though each separate defect was disposed of by his evasions. But, in point of fact, if the defects were viewed in their totality, the broker would have to agree that the girl was a rather poor marriage prospect: "He insisted on treating each defect in isolation and refused to add them up into a total."[30] The analogy would be a used-car salesman discounting a car's various defects noted by a wary customer, then responding to the customer's discovery that the engine is missing, "Well, what do you expect? After all, the car *is* used!" (or, as the modern euphemism has it, "pre-driven").

Freud notes that we find another piece of sophistry in the following marriage broker joke:[31]

> The would-be bridegroom complained that the prospective bride had one leg shorter than the other and limped. The marriage broker replied, "But just suppose you were to marry a woman with straight, healthy legs! What's the good of that? You'd never have a day of security that she wouldn't fall down, break a leg, and be lame for life. And think of the suffering, the agitation, and the doctor's bill! If you take this one, that can't happen to you. Here you have a *fait accompli*!

Freud points out that the appearance of logic is very thin in this joke, for "no one would prefer an already 'accomplished misfortune' to one that is merely a possibility."[32]

In the two marriage broker jokes cited so far, the broker discounts the defects pointed out by the prospective groom. In the following joke, the broker defeats his own objectives:[33]

> The prospective bridegroom was most disagreeably surprised when the prospective bride was introduced to him. Indignant, he drew the broker aside and whispered: "Why did you even bring me here? She's ugly and old, she squints and has bad teeth and bleary eyes…" The broker interrupted, "You don't have to lower your voice; she's deaf too."

Freud points out that the broker gets so caught up in "the enumeration of the bride's defects and infirmities that he completes the list out of his own knowledge, though this was certainly not his business or purpose."[34]

In this last joke, the sophistry—the misleading logic—in the two earlier ones is missing, and the marriage broker, against his own interests, reveals a defect that the prospective groom has not detected. Freud thinks that this disclosure invites us to seek out an even deeper truth that these marriage broker jokes only hint at: the typical suitor makes himself ridiculous when he enumerates all the advantages of the woman he intends to marry and forgets that she is "a human being with her inevitable defects."[35] Even more importantly, the very element that makes marriage between two imperfect individuals workable—their "mutual attraction and readiness for affectionate adaptation"—is completely missing from these accounts of the whole transaction.[36]

Thus, in Freud's view, what these jokes hint at by focusing on the people involved in the business of arranging a marriage—the broker, the bride, the bridegroom, and their parents—is that the very institution of arranged marriages is a sham. This brings us to one final marriage broker joke in which the broker, once again, defeats his own purposes:[37]

> The prospective bridegroom was paying his first visit to the prospective bride's house in the company of the broker. While they waited in the parlor for the family to appear, the broker drew attention to a cupboard with glass doors in which the finest set of china cups and plates were on full view. "Look at that! You can see from these things how rich these people are." The suspicious young man replied, "But isn't it possible these fine things were borrowed for the occasion to give the false impression of wealth?" The broker protested, "What an idea! Who do you think would lend these people anything?"

Here, just as in the previous joke, the broker gets "so carried away by his eagerness to convince the young man of the family's wealth that, in order to establish one confirmatory point, he brings up something that is bound to upset all his efforts."[38] Freud feels that in this joke, the implicit critique shifts from the marriage broker to the parents, who think that this deception on their part is "justified in order to get their daughter a husband, and upon the disgracefulness of marriages contracted on such a basis."[39] And no one is in better position to expose the disgracefulness of marriages contracted on such a basis than the broker, "for he knows most about these abuses; but he must not say them aloud, for he is a poor man whose existence depends on exploiting them."[40] Thus, these jokes, like the beggar jokes, address a conflict in the popular mind, which created these stories, concerning another sacred institution, for "it knows that the sacredness of marriages after they have been contracted is grievously affected by the thought of what happened at the time when they were arranged."[41]

Because the broker engages in faulty reasoning or sophistry in the first two of these jokes, the jokes are examples of the saving of expenditure in *difficult thinking*. One gets the sense that the marriage broker has become so accustomed to sophistry that he no longer knows what's true or false. But these jokes also illustrate the price paid by individuals for the community's *inhibitions*, in this case, the reluctance to acknowledge, much less speak out against, an abusive social institution. If marriages were blessed by rabbis, they were arranged by brokers, and these arrangements, besides being deceptive, take no account of the fundamental truth that what makes a marriage workable is the mutual attraction of the two persons entering into the marriage and their readiness to make affectionate adaptations to one another's inevitable defects. Freud believes that the primary function of jokes, only one of many forms of humor, arises from the economy in expenditure of costly inhibitions.[42] The beggar and marriage broker jokes presented in his book support this belief. Especially noteworthy is the fact that these two types of jokes break the taboo against criticizing two sacred institutions of the society in which they originate: the sacred duty of charity and the sacredness of the arranged marriage.

These marriage broker jokes may also enable an individual to gain distance or detachment from the *painful emotions* involved in the process of getting married in the first place. This is where Freud's personal interest in these jokes comes in. I suggest that by participating in the telling and hearing of these popular jokes, Freud would have gained a detachment from these emotions that he probably could not have realized in any other way. A five-year engagement? The opposition of his prospective bride's only living parent? Just the thing to laugh about! Maybe there is a lesson in this for anyone whose courtship was not entirely blissful: if the painful emotions of the past burden the present and the future, find yourself some marriage jokes and let them do their healing work. My aphorism would be: if you are psychologically broke, find yourself a saving joke!

Contemporary Role Models

Freud targeted his book on jokes to the era in which he lived, and the community to which he particularly belonged—hence, beggar and marriage broker jokes. We have our own jokes for *saving in the expenditure of painful emotions, costly inhibitions, and difficult thinking*: heartless lawyer jokes for *painful emotions*, foul-mouthed parrot jokes for *costly inhibitions*, and dumb blonde jokes for *difficult thinking*. After I present these three joke characters, I will discuss their implications for the Ministry of Good Humor, and explain why I consider them "role models," defined by *Webster's New World College Dictionary* as "a person who is unusually effective or inspiring in some social role, job, etc., and so serves as a model for another or others."[43] Let's begin with the lawyer jokes.

The Heartless Lawyer

Every general joke book that I possess, including one published in 1938,[44] contains lawyer jokes. Most have several dozen. One joke book is completely devoted to lawyer jokes; it is probably intended as a Christmas gift for the lawyer in your family.[45] If my purpose here were to demonstrate how jokes surreptitiously critique one of our own sacred institutions—the legal system—I would focus on jokes suggesting that our lawyers don't give a hoot about laws; they only care about making money.

My concern, rather, is with saving in the expenditure of *painful emotions*, with the fact that, according to lawyer jokes, lawyers are heartless. No heart, no pain. A stock lawyer joke that establishes this theme is that a heart transplant recipient has to pay a premium price for a lawyer's heart because, regardless of the lawyer's age when he died, it's still as good as new. But the following joke provides a specific illustration:

Mr. Graham was the chairman of the United Way. One day it came to his attention that the fund had never received a donation from the most successful lawyer in town. He called on the attorney, and confronted him: "Our research shows that you made a profit of over $600,000 last year. Yet you have not given a dime to the community charities. What do you have to say for yourself?" The lawyer replied, "Did your research also show that my mother is dying from a long illness, and has medical bills that are several times her annual income? Did your research uncover anything about my brother, the disabled veteran, who is blind and in a wheelchair? Do you know about my sister, whose husband died in a traffic accident, leaving her penniless with three children?" Sheepishly, the charity solicitor admitted that he had no knowledge of any of this. "Well, since I don't give any money to them, why should I give any to you?"

This joke recalls Freud's joke about the rich man who summoned his servants after listening to the beggar's tale of woe, saying, "Throw him out! He's breaking my heart!" This, though, is not about a beggar whom the benefactor may not even know. This is the lawyer's own family! The solicitor assumes, and so do we, that the lawyer would have had the decency to attend to their needs. The following joke suggests that a heartless lawyer's lack of feeling for his own kin knows no bounds:

A lawyer was approached by the Devil with a proposition. The Devil said he'd arrange for the lawyer to win every case, make twice as much money, work half as hard, be appointed to the Supreme Court Bench and live to age 95. In return, the lawyer had to promise the Devil the souls of his parents, his wife, and his three young children. The lawyer thought for a moment, then responded, "So what's the catch?"

If our heartless lawyer wasn't concerned that his family would burn in hell for all eternity, we aren't surprised that he would have no compassion for a group of blind golfers:

A minister, a doctor, and a lawyer were playing golf together one morning, but were stuck behind a particularly slow group. All three were complaining about how long the group was taking on each hole. Finally they spotted the greens keeper, so they decided to have a word with him. "That's a group of blind firefighters," he explained, "They lost their sight while saving our clubhouse last year. So we let them play here any time free of charge. The minister said, "That's so sad. I think I'll say a special prayer for them tonight." The doctor said, "That's a good idea, and I'm going to consult all my textbooks to see if there isn't something that can be done for them." The lawyer said, "Why can't these guys play at night?"

If these jokes suggest that the lawyer has no feelings whatsoever, the following joke takes exception to the view that he is totally devoid of feeling for another human being:

A lawyer comes to visit his client on death row and says, "I have some good news for you." The client responds, "What good news are you talking about? You lost my case, I was convicted of a murder I did not commit, and I've been sentenced to die in the electric chair!" The lawyer replied, "That's all true, but I got the voltage lowered."

In the next joke, the lawyer is positively filled with compassion for his client, and appeals to the jury for a similar act of compassion:

A lawyer, addressing the jury, spoke of his client who was on trial for killing his parents: "Dear ladies and gentlemen, I appeal to you to take mercy on this poor, unhappy orphan."

His appeal, based on a technicality, suggests that his expression of feeling for his client is insincere. A member of the jury might also point out to the others that his sympathy seems a bit misplaced. However sad the fate of the defendant, the fate of his parents seems a lot worse.

It's difficult to find any redeeming qualities in the joke character of the heartless lawyer. But let's not write him off too soon. We'll get back to him. Meanwhile, the foul-mouthed parrot is squawking for our attention.

The Foul-Mouthed Parrot

Let's turn to the savings in expenditure of *costly inhibitions*. It seems to say that our inhibitions fall into two general categories: things we try not to say and things we try not to do. Michael Billig suggests in his book, *Freudian Repression: Conversation Creating the Unconscious*,[46] that Freud was especially interested in inhibitions relating to what we say. We learn as small children to say some things ("You must say *please*") and not say other things ("That was a rude thing to say to your sister. Tell her that you didn't mean it").

As Billig points out, Freud knew that whenever we say one thing, we generally inhibit the saying of another thing. The "talking cure" Freud pioneered involved learning to actually say things that you thought, but that you knew would be resented, misconstrued, or have far-reaching consequences. In the psychoanalyst's office, you were instructed to engage in uninhibited talk, to say whatever came into your mind.

The parrot seems to exemplify the saving in the expenditure of this form of inhibition. He is a stock character in pirate books and movies. He hangs around pirates, who are the most foul-mouthed members of a profession—sailor—known for cussing and swearing. Being a creature of his environment, he is foul-mouthed too. He is foul-mouthed in jokes too. But in jokes, he learned to speak this way before he became the property of the current owner, so his present owner considers his language personally offensive and embarrassing, particularly when the owner is entertaining friends and other guests. The parrot also seems to go in for mockery. This, at least, is how it appears to the humans around him when he imitates their own pet sayings. The pet parrot of an elderly woman was accustomed to saying "helloooo" whenever the phone rang. But when a twenty-eight-year-old man rented a room in her apartment, the parrot added, "What's up, man?" to his ringing-phone repertoire.[47]

(The parrot also said, "Not to Worry," as though he knew anything about it.)

Here's an example of a parrot whose language was offensive to his new owner, and the owner tried to do something about it:

> Bob received a parrot for his birthday. The parrot was fully grown, with a bad attitude and worse vocabulary. Every other word was an expletive. Those that weren't expletives were, to say the least, rude. Bob tried hard to change the bird's attitude and was constantly saying polite words, playing soft music, doing anything he could think of to try to set a good example. Nothing worked. He yelled at the bird, and the bird got worse. He shook the bird, and the bird became even ruder. Finally, in a moment of desperation, Bob put the parrot in the freezer. For a few moments he heard the bird squawking and cursing—and then suddenly all was quiet. Bob was afraid that he had actually hurt the bird and quickly opened the freezer door. The parrot stepped out onto Bob's extended arm and said, "I'm sorry that I might have offended you with my language and actions and ask for your forgiveness. I will endeavor to correct my behavior." Bob was astonished at the bird's change in attitude and was about to ask what had made such a drastic change when the parrot said, "Sir, may I ask what the chicken did?"

The parrot appears to have undergone a remarkable transformation. But his formal speech ("I will endeavor to correct my behavior," and, "Sir, may I ask...") suggests a bit of obsequiousness, and this seems confirmed by his implied association of his own rather light punishment with the fate of the frozen, beheaded chicken.

Here's a joke about a parrot who makes Bob's bird seem almost saintly by comparison:

> When a rundown section of town was condemned, the goods from its various buildings were sold. This

included a parrot, who ended up in an exclusive pet store and was purchased by an affluent woman who belonged to the country-club set. Despite every effort, she was unable to get the parrot to talk. She coaxed it, offered it crackers, but the bird wouldn't say a word. One night the woman's bridge club was playing at her home, and the conversation turned to the comfort of their respective panty hose. Deciding to check the labels, they hitched up their designer dresses. "Finally," the bird squawked, "home sweet home. Now will one of you whores gimme a smoke?"

Both of these jokes illustrate the importance of early training, and the difficult of undoing the effects of a bad upbringing.

The following joke focuses on the theme, also evident in the "Bob's parrot" joke, that righteousness is often only skin deep:

A lady bought a parrot from a pet store, only to discover after bringing the bird home that it would say nothing but, "My name is Mary and I'm a whore." Weeks of trying to teach the bird other phrases proved hopeless. Furthermore, much to this respectable woman's embarrassment, the bird dropped the same line at the most inopportune moments. One day her parish priest dropped by for a visit and, sure enough, while he was there the parrot squawked out the only words it would say. The woman apologized to the priest, explaining that the parrot resisted all efforts at reformation. The priest offered to take the bird to visit his two parrots, as their vocal repertoire consisted entirely of Hail Marys while clutching rosaries in their talons. He was certain that they would have a good influence on the woman's parrot. So he took the parrot home and put it in the cage with the other birds, and, sure enough, the first words out of her mouth were, "My name is Mary and I'm a whore." Whereupon, one of the priest's parrots said to his companion, "Throw that rosary away! Our prayers have been answered!"

Parrots also tend to be rude to visitors. They can be more effective than dogs in protecting houses from unwelcome visitors. Here's an example:

A bill collector rapped on the front door and heard a faint, high-pitched, "Come in." He tried the door, but it was locked. So he went around to the back door. He knocked again and heard the same high-pitched, "Come in." It was unlocked, so he entered. A large, mean snarling Doberman met him in the hallway. As he plastered himself against the wall, he called for help. Again, he heard the same high-pitched voice, "Come in." He shouted, "For Pete's sake, is 'come in' all you can say?" The parrot in the cage in the kitchen replied brightly, "I can also say 'Sic 'im'!"

This parrot doesn't use foul language, but the combination of his welcoming and hostile language is just as bad, or worse.

In the following joke, the parrot doesn't even have to use hostile language to have a devastating effect on the visitor. All he needs to do is to feign interest in the identity of the caller:

A woman goes into a store and buys a beautiful green and blue parrot. But the only words the parrot knows how to say are, "Who is it?" She takes the parrot home. Later, her kitchen sink gets clogged and she calls the plumber. He says he'll come out later in the day, but can't say when, because he's had a couple of emergency calls that he has to handle first. When he knocks at the door, she is out shopping. The parrot calls out, "Who is it?" "It's the plumber." The parrot calls out again, "Who is it?" The plumber answers in a louder voice, "It's the plumber!" The parrot calls out again, "Who is it?" The plumber, exasperated, shouts, "It's the plumber!!" The parrot calls out,

"Who is it?" The plumber, angry now, hollers at the top of his voice, "IT'S THE PLUMBER!!" For a fifth time, the parrot calls out, "Who is it?" Before he can answer, the plumber clutches his heart and falls in a heap on the front porch, the victim of a heart attack brought on by his frustration and anger. The woman comes home and finds the dead man lying on her front porch. Aghast, she cries out, "Who is it?" The parrot replies, "It's the plumber."

The parrot's facility with the English language has doubled, but the price for this lesson in word acquisition seems unnecessarily high. The plumber is dead, and woe to the plumber who has the bad luck to receive the woman's second call.

Jokes about parrots tend to focus on the parrot's foul language. They assume, though, that behind the foul language is a bad attitude. Parrots in jokes are not mean or vicious, but they are smart-alecky, and they are disinclined to be respectful toward humans. Their vocabulary is generally limited, and this makes their use of expletives seem all the more offensive. In *Cuss Control: The Complete Book on How to Curb Your Cursing,* James V. O'Connor, the founder of the Cuss Control Academy, says, "Swearing is not the worst thing you can do, but you must be careful about when and where you swear to avoid offending others and appearing ignorant."[48] This ignorance derives from the fact that, as the *Washington Times* review of the book cited on the back cover puts it, "Swearing is not only bad manners, [O'Connor says], it's poor communication that shows a lack of imagination and a limited vocabulary." O'Connor also states, "Adults should have the maturity, vocabulary, and emotional control to avoid using profanity. They have a responsibility to show younger people how to communicate in a civilized manner."[49]

Notice O'Connor's observation that swearing is uncivilized. He is certainly right about this. On the other hand, Freud observes that an inevitable consequence of living in a civilized world is that we become inhibited, and that the inhibition has its own psychic costs. A good illustration of this is a revised version of the "My name is Mary and I'm a whore" joke previously presented above. This revision appears in *The Best Ever Book of Good Clean Jokes* by Bob Phillips:[50]

A dignified old clergyman owned a parrot of whom he was exceedingly fond, but the bird had picked up an appalling vocabulary of cuss words from a previous owner and, after a series of embarrassing episodes, the clergyman decided he would have to kill his pet. A lady in his parish suggested a last-ditch remedy. "I have a female parrot," she said, "who is an absolute saint. She sits quietly on her perch and says nothing but 'Let's pray.' Why don't you bring your parrot over and see if my own bird's good influence doesn't reform him." The clergyman said it was worth a trial, and the next night he arrived with his pet tucked under his arm. The bird took one look at the lady parrot and chirped, "Hi, toots. How about a little kiss?" "My prayers have been answered," said the lady parrot gleefully.

There's no doubt that this is a "cleaner" version of the joke. But I have to confess that I don't like it as much, partly because I find it confusing, and partly because it actually seems *less* moral than the other version. What's confusing to me is the fact that the parrot is said to have "an appalling vocabulary of cuss words," yet what he "chirped" to the female parrot—"Hi, toots. How about a little kiss?"—seems pretty innocuous. If this is an example of his appalling vocabulary, I'd say that the clergyman has set an impossibly high standard for what counts as acceptable speech. Or is the point that the female parrot has an immediate "good influence" on him, and, "Hi, toots. How about a little kiss?" is a sign of his reformation? If the latter, the meaning of the joke has taken an 180 degree turn. To me, it isn't funny anymore—cute, perhaps, but not funny. The second problem I have with the "clean" version is that it represents a man—a clergyman, no less—as planning to kill a bird because of his "appalling vocabulary." And why? Because the parrot has created "a series of embarrassing episodes" for its owner.

Doesn't this seem a bit extreme? It certainly would to the parrot who was placed in the freezer for a few moments and, when he got out, wondered what the chicken had done to warrant *his* fate. Moreover, it would have seemed equally extreme to Bob, the parrot's owner, who "was afraid he had actually hurt the bird and quickly opened the freezer door." But if I were a parrot—unregenerate or otherwise—I'd feel a lot safer with Bob than with the dignified old clergyman.

I'll eventually get back to the foul-mouthed parrot. In the meantime, the dumb blonde is waving her hand for our attention. She thinks it's her left hand, but the heartless lawyer knows she's mistaken about this. After all, he has watched thousands of witnesses raise their right hands and swear on the Bible. ("No, foul-mouthed parrot, not *your* kind of swearing").

The Dumb Blonde

The third saving in expenditure is in *difficult thinking.* Stupidity jokes are nothing new. In his book *Jokes and Their Relation to Society,* Christie Davies points out that the jokes told in Egypt about the simple, weak-minded Nubians who live in the rural southern region of Egypt are thousands of years old.[51] So, in the beginning, stupidity jokes reflected an urban bias against rural people, who were considered provincial and backward. Davies thinks, though, that the rising popularity of stupidity jokes in the last century has more to do with the highly rationalized nature of modern society, especially in the workplace. The specialization and division of labor make individuals anxious because they know and understand only a small fraction of the whole enterprise in which they are involved. At one extreme are the highly specialized who cannot afford to make mistakes (think brain surgeons) and at the other extreme are those who perform simple, repetitive tasks that require hardly any skill or intelligence at all (think janitors). Both are subject to stress, the former because of the pressures involved, the latter because they are expendable. Stupidity jokes, Davies suggests, help us deal with these anxieties.[52]

The dumb blonde would neither understand nor care to understand the last paragraph. As we begin to focus on blonde jokes, it's important to know that the joke world has two conflicting views of what is going on the head of a dumb blonde. One is that there isn't much going on ("What do you call it when a blonde is grabbing at air? Collecting her thoughts"). The other is that there's a lot going on, but you really don't want to know what it is. The majority of the jokes reflect the second view, and the following jokes are of this sort.

One of the hallmarks of dumb blonde jokes is that they violate the simple rules of rational thinking. Here's an example of faulty sequential thinking:

> A young blonde woman is distraught because she fears her husband is having an affair, so she goes to a gun shop and buys a handgun. The next day she comes home to find her husband in bed with a beautiful redhead. She grabs the gun and holds it to her own head. The husband leaps out of bed, pleading, "Don't do this to yourself!" She replied, "My mind is made up! And you're next!"

Here's an example of an inappropriate inference:

> Two blondes boarded an airplane. Fifteen minutes into the flight, the pilot announced: "One of the engines has failed and I'm sorry to say that the flight will be an hour longer; but don't be concerned, we have three engines left." Fifteen minutes later, he announced: "Our second engine has failed, so I regret to tell you that the flight will be two hours longer." Fifteen minutes elapsed, and the captain came on the intercom again: "It seems our third engine has failed. This means it will take an additional hour to complete our flight." One blonde turned to the other and moaned, "If we lose another engine, we'll be up here all day!"

In the following joke, the dumb blonde makes an inappropriate inference based, evidently, on her belief that the man on the bridge wouldn't make the same mistake twice:

> A blonde and a redhead met in a bar after work for a drink, and were watching the six o'clock news. A man

was shown threatening to jump from the Brooklyn Bridge. The blonde bet the redhead $50 that the guy wouldn't jump, and the redhead replied, "I'll take that bet!" The man jumped, so the blonde paid up. The redhead said, "I can't take this, you're my friend." The blonde said, "No, a bet's a bet." So the redhead said, "Really, I can't take you're money. I saw this story on the five o'clock news." The blonde replied, "Well, so did I, but I never thought he'd jump again!"

The following airplane joke indicates that the dumb blonde is not so set in her ways that she will not listen to an appeal based on reason rather than mere coercion:

A blonde gets on an airplane and sits down in the first-class section. The flight attendant tells her she must move to the coach section because she doesn't have a first-class ticket. The blonde replies, "I'm blonde, I'm smart, I have a good job, and I'm staying in first class until we reach Jamaica." The flight attendant gets the head flight attendant who asks her to leave. She repeats, "I'm blonde, I'm smart, I have a good job, and I'm staying in first class until we reach Jamaica." The flight attendants don't know what to do because the rest of the passengers need to be seated, so they summon the co-pilot. He goes up to her and whispers in her ear. She immediately gets up and goes to her seat in the coach section. The head flight attendant asks him what he said to get her to move. He replies, "I told her that the front half of the airplane wasn't going to Jamaica."

All she needed was an appeal to her rational mind and the flight crew's dilemma was solved.

The following joke will take us full circle, for the guy in the joke is a lawyer, and he thinks he can get some easy money out of a blonde because, after all, blondes are dumb and lawyers are smart:

A lawyer and a blonde were sitting in a bar. All the blonde wanted to do was to sip her drink and give her mind a rest. But the lawyer saw the chance to make some easy money. He said, "Let's play a game. I ask you a question, and if you don't know the answer, you pay me $5, and vice versa." She replied, "No, I don't want to have to think." The lawyer persisted, figuring that taking money from a blonde would be like taking candy from a baby: "I'll tell you what. If you don't know the answer, you only pay me $5, and if I don't know the answer, I'll pay you $50." She replied, "O.K., if it makes you happy." The lawyer asked the first question: "What's the circumference of the earth?" The blonde didn't even try to think, but just handed over the $5. Now it was her turn: "What goes up a hill with three legs and comes back with four?" He was stumped. He couldn't believe that she could come up with a question he couldn't answer. He asked her if he could use his computer to e-mail some friends and check the Internet. "Why not?" she replied, as she sipped her drink. After a half hour of consultation and research, he finally had to admit defeat. He handed her the $50. "So what's the answer?" he asked. "Beats me," she replied, as she handed him another $5.

I rather like this joke because I wanted her to win. The joke invites us to ask just who the dumb one is. The blond has come up with what seems to be a riddle, one not unlike the famous riddle of the Sphinx: "What goes on four legs in the morning, two legs in the afternoon, and three legs in the evening?" Answer: a human being, who crawls in infancy, walks upright as an adult, and uses a cane in old age. But her riddle has no answer—just what the scheming, heartless lawyer deserves.

Our dumb blonde would never be accused of "over-thinking," the problem that Susan Nolen-Hoeksema addresses in her book *Women Who Think Too Much: How to Break Free of Over-thinking and Reclaim Your Life*.[53] Nolen-Hoeksema carefully distinguishes "over-thinking" from worry, noting that where worriers spend tremendous energy anticipating everything that could possibly go wrong, over-thinkers dwell on the past—"events that have happened, things you have done, situations you wish had gone differently."[54] Nor is over-thinking to be confused with obsessive-compulsive disorder or genuinely "deep thinking." She identifies three types of over-thinking: (1) *rant and rave* (thinking about some wrong one believes has been done to oneself and ending up with thoughts of how to get even); (2) *life-of-their-own* (thinking about a recent event that begins innocently enough and then escalates to the point where implausible meanings predominate over plausible ones); and (3) *chaotic over-thinking* (thinking that does not move in a straight line from one problem to the next, but rather all sorts of unrelated concerns flood one's mind all at once). The studies that Nolen-Hoeksema has conducted over a couple of decades show that over-thinking makes life harder in the sense that the stresses we face seem bigger and good solutions become more elusive; relationships are hurt because our over-thinking is annoying to others; and over-thinking may even contribute to mental disorders, including depression, severe anxiety, and alcohol abuse.[55]

Considering the negative effects of over-thinking, one has to wonder how the blonde in the joke world came to be thought of as dumb. Even her response when she notices a banana peel on the sidewalk in front of her—"Here we go again"—makes a great deal of sense. I realized this after I had taken a rather bad fall on a sidewalk where the pavement was uneven, and recalled that I had done the very same thing in the very same place a few months earlier. The allegedly *dumb* blonde, then, gets it right: "Here we go again" is the story of our lives.

Implications for the Ministry of Good Humor

What do the heartless lawyer, the foul-mouthed parrot, and the dumb blonde have to teach us, this rag-tag assemblage of old believers and recent converts to the Ministry of Good Humor? More specifically, how can they possibly be viewed as positive role models whom we would bid those who require our ministry to emulate? My answer will need to be suggestive only, but I assume that anyone who has had the wisdom to join our ranks in the first place will have no difficulty in filling in the blanks. I'll take them up one at a time.

The Heartless Lawyer and the Cost of Painful Emotions

Suppose that a woman you know—say, a colleague, a parishioner, or a student—tells you the following story:

> My younger sister is going through a horrendous divorce, and she's having such a hard time of it. We've been such good friends from childhood, and I know that she has always looked up to me, her older sister. Our parents don't understand why she's divorcing her husband, and our brother is so distant, and this leaves me as the only one in the family whom she can confide in. I'm worried sick about her, and her troubles have been on my mind so much these past few weeks that it's affecting my work, my eating habits, and even my sleep. And I used to be such a sound sleeper. Oh, how my heart goes out to her.

Obviously, a sensitive Minister of Good Humor would not immediately respond, "Hey, that reminds me of a joke. Have you heard the one about the divorce court judge who said to the husband…":

> "Mr. Geraghty, I have reviewed this case carefully and I've decided to give your wife $800 dollars a week." "That's very fair, your honor," he replied, "And every now and then I'll try to send her a few bucks myself."

Besides the poor timing involved, this joke could lead to a discussion of how jokes trade on linguistic contrivances, like "I've decided to give…," or the many versions of the joke in which a guy who goes up to the piano player in the bar and says, "Do you know your fly is open?" or, "Do you know your monkey spit in my beer?" and the piano player replies, "Not offhand, could you hum a few bars?" or "Know it? I *wrote* it!" This is certainly not the direction you want the conversation to take.

More useful, though, would be to reflect on her comment that her heart goes out to her sister and on the effects that her sister's troubles are having on her concentration at work, her eating, her sleeping. Now is the time to respond sympathetically to her, the woman who is sitting there in the room. Hopefully, there are others who will care for her sister. Having identified the focus of *your own concern*, her words, "My heart goes out to my sister," remind you of a guy whose heart goes out to no one—the heartless lawyer, the guy whose heart is so valuable to organ recipients because it is brand spanking new. She needs this fictional lawyer's help in the same way that her sister needs the assistance of a divorce lawyer. He will help her get some of her heart back so that her life can return to normal. Her poor concentration at work, her disrupted eating habits and sleeping patterns are concrete, empirical evidence that she is living beyond her psychological means, and that she desperately needs to save in her current expenditure of painful emotions.

Do you mention the heartless lawyer to her? Do you tell her that *she* needs to consult a lawyer, and that you know just the one she needs to consult? I would think not. We all know that the heartless lawyer is no saint. He was never a candidate for inclusion in Sean Kelly and Rosemary Rogers' *Saints Preserve Us! Everything You Need to Know About Every Saint You'll Ever Need.*[56] Because he is no saint, one would not want to emulate him, or model one's life after him. But the Ministry of Good Humor is a modest undertaking. In fact, it deliberately sets its sights rather low so that it will be able to live up to its own expectations of itself. Another minister might have suggested to the woman that she needed to consult a therapist to help her through this difficult time, and maybe this minister would have been right to do so. But there is something a bit counterintuitive about recommending a heartless lawyer in a case of the overspending of painful emotions, and all the Ministers of Good Humor whom I have had the pleasure to meet would drink to that!

The Foul-Mouthed Parrot and Costly Inhibitions

Having convinced all but the most skeptical reader that the heartless lawyer is a good role model, I will now make a similar case on behalf of the foul-mouthed parrot. Supposing that a man you know tells you the following story:

> My boss is the most irritating creature on the face of this earth. She gives us all a lot of meaningless busy work, and she herself is so wrapped up in busy work that she doesn't know the difference between productive work and the appearance of working. What especially galls me is that her superiors think she is doing a great job, when I know full well that our unit is floundering around, doing nothing worthwhile. I'd quit in a minute but I'm too young to retire and too old to go out looking for another job.

An insensitive Minister of Good Humor might respond, "Hey, speaking of work problems, I'll bet you haven't heard this one":

> A guy had a problem getting up for work in the morning and was frequently reprimanded for being late. It got so bad that he went to see a doctor who gave him a pill to take at bedtime. After taking the pill, the guy slept soundly, woke up refreshed, had a leisurely breakfast and went to work. "Hi, I feel great," he told the boss. "I think all my timekeeping problems are a thing of the past." "That's wonderful to hear," the boss replied, "But where were you yesterday?"

No, this is not the way to do it. Even the *inexperienced* Minister of Good Humor would know this, and might take a more sensible approach: "Why don't you tell her how you feel? You might be surprised at her response. Lots of people have changed their ways of doing things. She could very well be one of them." This would only elicit the response: "But her superiors like the way she's doing things. Do you seriously think she would change just to accommodate me? No, she'd humor me, and go on her merry way, just the same as ever."

Experienced Ministers of Good Humor wouldn't waste their time in this way. Instead, they'd scratch their heads and say to themselves, "What do I have in my bag of tricks that could possibly help this guy?" Then, light bulbs appear above their heads with the accompanying caption, "The foul-mouthed parrot!" This guy's problem is that he is spending psychological resources he doesn't even have on costly inhibitions. He should instead be spending his money on fees for a workshop taught by the foul-mouthed parrot. As we have seen, the foul-mouthed parrot had a rather uncivilized upbringing, but he is not about to adapt to the civilized world of which he has become a member through not fault of his own. Instead, he will put the burden back on those who are seeking to recreate him in their own image, or, as they so quaintly put it, to "reform" him. But he will have none of this. He likes himself the way he is, and who are they to define what makes an "ideal" parrot?

Do you mention the foul-mouthed parrot to the guy with the problem? I don't think so. He might take it the wrong way, especially since he seems to be the kind of guy who would try to reform the parrot. No, the idea is that the parrot is helping *you* with *your* problem, which is that of helping him.

Of all the foul-mouthed parrots we have reviewed, I would take Bob's parrot as the best role model. Bob works diligently to make him toe the line, but his efforts fail. He takes the more drastic measure of putting the parrot into the freezer, but all that this accomplishes is that the parrot changes—temporarily, we would assume—from the foul-mouthed parrot to the obsequious parrot: offering apologies and speaking deferentially in a manner that his owner has no choice but to accept at face value.

How the guy who works for an "irritating creature" of a boss will adapt the things he learns from the parrot's workshop may require a bit of brainstorming, for every work situation is different. But he would quit spending psychological resources he doesn't have so that he can go to work with an unmortgaged future. Maybe he will go through the motions of reformation, doing the busy work as if he thinks it has some value, or, alternatively, pretending that he has reviewed, assimilated, and processed the busy work while, in fact, giving the lion's share of his attention to projects that he knows are truly valuable.

Instead of even thinking about leaving to go elsewhere, he would remind himself that he is a parrot, not a chicken, and parrots have their pride to consider. The Minister of Good Humor might even avail *himself* of the tradition in whose service he labors, and cite the unfortunate case of Peter Abelard (1079–1142), who was emasculated at the instigation of his lover Heloise's uncle, and, at the early age of thirty-nine, left his teaching post to enter a monastery. As if this were not bad enough, when he left one monastery and joined another, he lamented that in "seeking to shun threats I fled to a certain peril."[57] I ask you: Would our foul-mouthed, unregenerate parrot voluntarily move from Bob's apartment to the home of the old, dignified clergyman? No way. He would be the first to discern that behind the clergyman's fondness for him lurked a deeper willingness to do away with his parrot if he would not conform to the clergyman's civilized ways.

I can well imagine that some readers will protest, "But what you are suggesting or implying is not the Christian way." We could debate this point, and if we did, I would probably invoke our Lord Jesus' allusion to the wisdom of serpents and innocence of doves in the midst of wolves (Mt. 10:16), as if to say that we cannot be much use to him if we don't take care of ourselves. I might also toss in his warning about wolves masquerading in sheep's clothing (Mt. 7:15). But we're talking here about the foul-mouthed parrot as a resource for a beleaguered man, not as a model for the entirety of one's life and one's manner of being in the world. This man has been overspending his psychological capital, and he needs to cut back. In this sense, he is insufficiently conservative where his psychological resources are concerned, and the parrot is here to tell him that there are ways to be free despite the fact that you are confined to an iron cage. And this brings us to our third role model, the dumb blonde.[58]

The Dumb Blonde and Difficult Thinking

I already have said some good things about the dumb blonde, but have not yet shown how she might be a positive role model in the Ministry of Good Humor. The question is how she may play a vital role in saving in the expenditure of difficult thinking. Supposing that someone you know tells you the following story:

> My parents are in their eighties and, being the sibling who lives nearest to where they live, I'm the one they are counting on to help them figure out what to do. They know they can't live in their home much longer. My dad can't handle the yard work and won't pay to have it done, and my mom can't do the housework any longer but doesn't want a housekeeper to come in and do it because she doesn't think it will be done right and worries that the housekeeper will pilfer her jewelry and help herself to the food in the refrigerator. They are resigned to having to sell the house and move into some kind of retirement center or community, but I've taken them to look at the ones in the vicinity of their home, and they have objected to all of them. Either they are too expensive, too regimented, or too far from the shopping mall. Nothing seems to suit them. I'm racking my brains as to what more I can do.

The insensitive Minister of Good Humor might respond, "Speaking of old parents," then proceed to tell this one: "My grandmother started walking five miles a day when she was sixty. She's ninety-seven today, and we haven't the foggiest idea where she is." But you, of course, are not the insensitive type. Nonetheless, you can readily see that this is going to be a tough case. In fact, you also begin to rack your brain, trying to think of something she may not have tried with her parents. But you can't think of anything. You are just as stymied as she is. What to say to her?

Then the dumb blonde begins to whisper in your ear: "Give your mind a rest and tell her to do the same." Because you know this advice is coming from a *dumb* blonde, you don't trust it at first. But then you begin to realize that one thing the dumb blonde hasn't done is to overspend her psychological resources as far as difficult thinking is concerned. No. In fact, she has amassed a huge savings account that could come in handy someday, though it's hard to imagine that she will ever need it. So maybe she has something there. At least, it's worth a try. So you say to the woman, "Mary, you've done all that you can for them. So give your mind a rest." If you feel it would help to add something biblical, you could say, "You've planted a seed, now let it grow of its own accord" (see Mk 4: 26- 29).

Should you mention the dumb blonde to her? I certainly wouldn't. I have yet to meet a woman who would appreciate someone saying to her, "I know a dumb blonde who could teach you some important lessons in life." No, as with the heartless lawyer and the foul-mouthed parrot, keep it to yourself. Like a good detective questioning suspects, good psychotherapists do not reveal all their methods to their clients, and neither should Ministers of Good Humor. Only you know that the woman who has taken back a big part of her mind has a dumb blonde to thank for this. And only you know that these three joke characters help explain why a substantial part of your own heart, soul, and mind are not in hock to creditors, and are therefore available for you to minister to others.

4

Aging, Illness, and Death

"A Time to Weep/A Time to Laugh"

This is a chapter I would prefer not to have to write, but a handbook for Ministers of Good Humor that does not address the issues of aging, illness, and death would not be worth the paper it is printed on. The quotation in the chapter title is from Ecclesiastes, which tells us, "for everything there is a season, and a time for every matter under heaven." There is "a time to be born, and a time to die; a time to plant, and a time to pluck up what is planted; a time to kill, and a time to heal; a time to break down, and a time to build up; *a time to weep, and a time to laugh*" (Eccl. 3:1-4, emphasis added). Given its inclusion in this recital of contrasting events, "a time to weep, and a time to laugh" conveys the impression that these, too, are very distinct occasions. Yet I suspect that all of us have had experiences when we didn't know whether to laugh or cry.

A friend tells me that he officiated at a funeral where the deceased man's wife laid her head on the lid of the casket and broke into uncontrollable laughter. You thought, of course, that I was about to say uncontrollable sobbing or weeping. But in *Laughter: A Scientific Investigation*, Robert R. Provine points out that, "Although laughter and crying are considered polar opposites of the emotional spectrum, they are neurologically linked," and share the features of breaking into tears and rhythmic vocalization.[1] This observation occurs in his chapter on "abnormal and inappropriate laughter," and, no doubt, the woman's laughter at her husband's funeral was both abnormal and inappropriate. But the idea that laughter might take the place of crying is well worth thinking about as we focus on the three issues of aging, illness, and death.

I will discuss aging first, illness second, and death third. I might mention here, at the outset, that the first letters of these three concerns make the word *aid*, so it might appropriate to say that humor's role is to offer *first aid* (the first letters of the words, "funny is required some times," spell *first*).

All the topics covered in this book have as much relevance for laity as for clergy. But this chapter seems especially suited for the laity. The clergy are often so involved in the planning of worship services, educational programming, committee work, and other leadership responsibilities, that they may not have the opportunity to devote as much time to the aging, the ill, and the dying as they wish they could. Of course, some clergy work full-time with the aging, the ill, and the dying, as hospital chaplains, or in hospice programs and retirement centers. They are doing wonderful work. A friend who was a seminary professor throughout his professional life commented to me when we were talking about a chaplain with whom we were both acquainted: "He humbles me." Still, there are limits to what chaplains can do for those who are ill or dying, and for their families, for a significant part of their work is in training seminary students and the ordained clergy in hospital ministry, and in serving as pastor to the hospital staff. So this chapter is written especially with the laity in mind.

I am aware, though, that there are many excellent programs and workbooks for lay ministry with the aging, the ill, and the dying. So there isn't much point in my duplicating what is already available. Instead, my goal is far more modest: I want to make a case for humor as a ministerial agent in connection with aging, illness, and death. Humor doesn't have the miraculous powers ascribed, say, to the relics of saints, but if appropriate to the situation and timely, it can function in the way that Proverbs 12:25 envisions: "Anxiety weighs down the human heart, / but a good word cheers it up." Let's see what this might mean for the aging process.

Humor and the Aging Process

From the time we are born, we begin to age. Aging, then, is something we are doing all the time, and whenever it occurs, it has effects. There are periods in our lives, though, when the aging process especially draws attention to itself because it seems to be working against the smooth functioning of the body. Adolescence is one of those times. The years from about the mid-sixties or seventies to the time of death are another.

Integrity vs. Despair

Because I encountered his writings at a time when I was trying to figure myself out—mid-twenties—I have been a lifelong fan of Erik H. Erikson. He is best known for his theory that our lives comprise eight ages or stages, and for his idea that each of these stages involves a dynamic interaction between two poles—one positive, one negative—and that the ideal is to maintain a certain "ratio" in which the positive qualities predominate over the negative ones.[2]

I want to comment briefly on the eighth stage of "old age" with the dynamic interaction of *integrity vs. despair*. *Vital Involvement in Old Age* by Erik H. Erikson, Joan M. Erikson, and Helen O. Kivnick describes the results of a study of twenty-nine older persons between the ages of seventy-five to ninety-five.[3] In Erikson's formulation of the *integrity vs. despair* dynamic, *integrity* has the following attributes: (1) an acceptance of one's one and only life cycle as something that had to be and that, by necessity, permitted no substitutions; (2) a sense of one's participation in the succession of generations; and (3) a maturity of life that reflects all the qualities or strengths of the earlier stages, now integrated into a more congruent whole. *Despair* has the following characteristics: (1) a fear of death that mainly derives from the inability to accept the life that one has lived; (2) the feeling that the time is now too short for the attempt to begin another life and to try out alternate roads to integrity; (3) it sometimes hides behind a show of disgust, misanthropy, and contempt for other persons and institutions; and (4) it may also be reflected in a self-contempt that is due to feeling little sense of comradeship with those whose lives and achievements mirror human dignity and love.

Erikson ascribed certain human strengths to each of the eight stages,[4] and assigned *wisdom* to the stage of old age. The key characteristics of wisdom are: (1) ripened wits, accumulated knowledge, matured judgment; (2) maintaining and conveying the integrity of experience; (3) vigor of mind combined with responsible renunciation; (4) the provision of the coming generation with an integrated heritage and living example of one who experienced its essential integrity; (5) the transcendence of petty disgusts and despair of becoming helpless; and (6) being in possession of a few things that offer confirmation.[5]

The study of the twenty-nine older persons found substantial evidence of both *integrity* and *despair*. It isn't easy to summarize the findings of the study, but these are some of the things that gave evidence of *integrity*:

1. Relying on the wisdom of the elders whom they had held in highest regard in their earlier years, such as a grandparent or an aging parent, or another older person whom they admired, such as a celebrity, a neighbor, or a good Samaritan at a seniors' center.

2. Increased concern for and tolerance of the world and its multifarious inhabitants, reflected in greater patience, open-mindedneess, understanding, compassion, and ability to see "both sides" of an issue. An awareness of the fact that one is "more set in one's ways" may not be inconsistent with this greater tolerance, for insistence on one's own preferred ways of doing things may make one more tolerant of other people when *they* insist on doing things their own way.

3. Developing a philosophy of aging, which includes continuing to grow and not allowing oneself to stagnate, energetic commitment to a daily routine, remaining actively involved with other people, acting on one's need to be needed, and maintaining a sense of humor, especially about oneself.

4. A turn to religion, including recollection of engagement in religious observances as a child, attending church, or affirming the importance of the ritualized community that churches represent.
5. Acknowledging and accepting one's past choices. This may include ascribing new meaning to earlier experiences that were painful or accepting the fact that earlier decisions cannot be altered now.
6. Integrating legitimate feelings of cynicism and hopelessness into a larger perspective that is more fundamentally accepting and hopeful.

If these were evidence of *integrity*, what were the grounds these older persons had for *despair*? There seem to have been six of these as well:

1. The fact that others their age are leaving the community— town, neighborhood, churches, organizations, clubs, etc.— in which they have spent much of their lives together.
2. Largely involuntary thoughts about dying, not feeling well, getting depressed, and feeling "somehow let down."
3. Necessary thinking about the future occurring in the context of the recognition that death may not be far off.
4. The perception that the future of the world is not as good as the past, together with the realization that one cannot do much about it.
5. Ruminating over one's earlier powerlessness to save a loved one from dying and thinking of what one might have done differently.
6. Being obligated to provide material assistance to family members when they should be capable of taking care of their own affairs.

Finally, there was much evidence of strategies that helped to maintain the predominance of integrity over despair. We might call these expressions of wisdom in action:

1. Taking a viable future for granted by involving oneself in activities that assume one has several or many productive years ahead.

2. Taking interest in one's grandchildren as representatives of a future that not only extends beyond one's own future but also that of one's own children.
3. Emulating an older person, especially a family member, who exemplified mental vigor and emotional strength when he or she was one's current age.
4. "Revising" the past by minimizing or even seeming to ignore the painful experiences or questionable decisions in earlier stages of life. (They were the parents of teenage children in a longitudinal study begun in 1929. So their responses could be compared with the extensive files on their children.)

This fourth strategy may appear to be a form of selective memory, but Ben Furman and Tapani Ahola make the following observation in their chapter, "The Role of the Past," in *Solution Talk: Hosting Therapeutic Conversations*:

> Our history is an integral part of ourselves. As long as we think of the past as the source of our problems, we set up, in a sense, an adversarial relationship within ourselves. The past, very humanly, responds negatively to criticism and blaming but favorably to respect and stroking. The past prefers to be seen as a resource, a store of memories, good and bad, and a source of wisdom emanating from life experience.[6]

Furman and Tapani recommend the therapeutic strategy of interpreting events in the past that were considered negative at the time in a more positive way, noting that "the view that past traumatic experiences are a source of problems in later life is certainly plausible," but "the opposite view that past ordeals are valuable learning experiences is equally sensible."[7]

Sense of Humor About Oneself

You probably noticed that a sense of humor, especially about oneself, was one of a handful of elements of an older person's "philosophy of aging." There are many ways in which this sense of humor might be cultivated, but certainly one of the more effective ones is to develop an appreciation for jokes about older persons.[8]

Jokes about older persons cover a range of topics and themes, but among the most common are themes of memory loss, mental confusion, hearing loss, loneliness, energy loss, changes in sexual activity, urinary problems, and driving habits.[9] I won't try to cover all of these bases here. Instead, I'll provide a small sampling of jokes on the aging adventures of older men. Here's a joke about memory loss:

> An old guy is sitting in the doctor's office waiting for the doctor to come in. When the doctor appears and asks him what seems to be the problem, he replies, "I think I'm losing my memory." The doctor asks, "When did this begin to happen?" He responds, "When did what begin to happen?"

Mental confusion is reflected in the joke about a guy who tells another guy: "My teeth are gone, my digestion's a mess, my joints ache, but at least my mind's still there, knock on wood. (KNOCKS) Who's there?" Here's another on mental confusion:

> The wives of three old men thought they should have their mental competency tested. The doctor who conducted the tests was very busy that morning, so he decided to test all three at once. He asked the first old guy, "What is two times two?" "194," came the reply. The doctor turned to the second old guy, "What is two times two?" "Thursday," he replied. Finally, the doctor addressed the third old guy. "What is two times two?" "Four," came the answer. "That's great," said the doctor, "How did you get that?" "Simple," he answered, "I subtracted 194 from Thursday!"

There are lifestyle issues associated with getting older, and one of these is loneliness: An old guy's wife asks, "Why are you sitting in the living room with no clothes on?" He answered, "Well, nobody's going to come visit me so what does it matter?" "Then you might as well remove your hat."

Energy loss is also an issue:

> An old guy went to his doctor and complained that
> he was unable to do things around the house that he
> used to do. After the doctor completed a thorough
> exam, the man said, "OK, Doc, I can take it. Tell me
> in plain English what's wrong with me." "All right,"
> the doctor replied, "in plain English, you're just lazy."
> "OK," he said, "Now tell me the medical term so I
> can tell my wife."

Many jokes about older persons focus on sexual issues.
Loss of sexual potency is a common theme, but so is
astonishing sexual potency (the latter of which recalls the
biblical story of Abraham and Sarah in Gen. 17—18):

> An old guy goes to the doctor for a physical. The
> doctor tells him he's in great shape for a 60-year-old.
> The old guy replies, "Who says I'm 60? I turn 80 next
> month." The doctor is surprised, "Gosh, 80! Then
> how old was your father when he died?" The old guy
> replies, "Who says he's dead? He's 105." The doctor
> responded, "With such a good family medical history,
> your grandfather must have been pretty old when he
> died." The old guy answered, "Who says he's dead?
> He'll be 129 in a couple of months, and he's getting
> married next week." The doctor exclaims, "That's
> amazing! But why would he want to get married at
> his age?" The old guy replied, "Who says he wants
> to?"[10]

Desire Never Fails

The fact that his grandfather is getting married at age
128 brings us to an issue that is hardly mentioned in the
study of the twenty-nine older persons. This is the fact that,
whatever else they may lose, older persons do not lose their
desire. Desire, as *Webster's New World Dictionary* notes, is
interchangeable with words like *wish*, or *want*, or *crave* in
the sense of "to long for," but more than these other words,
desire "stresses intensity or ardor."[11]

One evening while I was reading *The Norton Book of Light Verse*, I came across an old poem titled "Authorship" by James B. Naylor (1860-1945):[12]

> King David and King Solomon
> Led merry, merry lives,
> With many, many lady friends,
> And many, many wives;
> But when old age crept over them,
> With many, many qualms,
> King Solomon wrote the Proverbs,
> And King David wrote the Psalms.

I grudgingly admitted to myself that Naylor's poem was clever, but because I had been struggling of late with the fact that old age was also creeping over me, I set to work on a poem of dissent. I felt that my best case would be Solomon, whose very name is synonymous with wisdom, the human strength that, as we have seen, Erik Erikson assigned to those who have reached the "old age" stage of life. I titled my poem "The Canonical King":

> Solomon wrote his Proverbs
> As a young precocious sage,
> Then penned Ecclesiastes
> In cynical middle age.
> But old age brought him wisdom,
> Which inspired Songs on Sex.
> And this concludes my lecture
> On the works of Solomon Rex.

When I tried out my poem on the students in my course on poetry and the care of souls, I received further support for my thesis that Solomon penned Ecclesiastes in cynical middle age. A student provided me with a few pages from Leland Ryken's Words of Delight: A Literary Introduction to the Bible.[13] Ryken explains that Ecclesiastes 12:1–7 (which begins with the famous admonition "Remember your creator in the days of your youth, before the days of trouble come, and the years draw near when you will say, 'I have no pleasure in them'") is about old age. Descriptions of how the sun, moon and stars are darkened refer to weak eyesight; the clouds that return after the rain refer to tears from eyestrain; the keepers of the house that tremble are shaking hands and arms; the strong men that are bent depict stooping shoulders; the grinders that cease because they are few refer to loss of teeth; the windows that are dimmed refer to weak eyes; the doors on the street that are shut refer to weak hearing; the almond tree that blossoms indicates white hair; and the grasshopper that drags itself along refers to the loss of sprightliness in walking.[14]

One might conclude from this rather dismal account of old age that Solomon is describing his experience of being an old man himself. But this is not true. The clue to the fact that he is a middle-aged man portraying a stage in life he has observed but not experienced himself is the phrase that follows "the grasshopper drags itself along," to which he adds *"and desire fails"* (v. 5, emphasis added). Song of Solomon, which could not have been written prior to his sixtieth birthday, corrects this grievous error, for we who are older know that desire is the one thing that does not fail, and Song of Solomon is all about desire.

I admit that one *could* read Song of Solomon as a poem about young love, noting, for example, that in 5:11 the beloved's "locks are wavy, black as a raven," which contrasts with the "blossoming almond tree" of Ecclesiastes 12:5. But this is just the point. As Louise Gluck says in her poem, "Vespers," which might be said to be about the "evening" of life, "I was not a child: I could take advantage of illusions."[15] In other words, at my age, I can look in the mirror and see a head of hair that resembles either the "blossoming almond tree" *or* "wavy locks as black as a raven." It's entirely up to me, and what will decide the matter is not factual accuracy, but sheer desire. This is what Gluck means by taking advantage of illusions.

To prove my theory that Song of Solomon is the work of an old man, I clambered into bed and said to my wife (quoting Song 6:6): "Your teeth are like a flock of ewes, / that have come up from the washing; / all of them bear twins, / and not one among them is bereaved." "You say such sweet nothings," she murmured. As she snuggled into my arms, I imagined that she was thinking to herself, "I am my beloved's, / and his desire is for me" (7:10). As I lay there, these words came floating through the open window, "The flowers appear on the earth; / the time of singing has come, / and the voice of the turtledove / is heard in our land" (2:12). As *Webster's New World College Dictionary* points out, the turtledove is "any of several Old World wild doves noted for their plaintive cooing, and the affection that the mates are traditionally thought of as showing toward each other."[16]

We are "Old World" all right. No denying it. But we old people are also "wild doves," and what others may hear as tremulous snoring sounds are, to us, the melodious trill of plaintive cooing. There is a time to jabber and yammer, and there is a time to sing, and ours is the time for singing. But I am among the newly old as I write this, so I would like to conclude this meditation on desire with a poem titled "Touch Me" by Stanley Kunitz, who was at least 90 years old when he wrote it.[17] The first line is from a poem, "As Flowers Are," which he had written forty years earlier:

> *Summer is late, my heart,*
> Words plucked out of the air
> some forty years ago
> when I was wild with love
> and torn almost in two
> scatter like the leaves this night
> of whistling wind and rain.
> It is my heart that's late,
> it is my song that's flown.
> Outdoors all afternoon
> under a gunmetal sky
> staking my garden down,
> I kneeled to the crickets trilling
> underfoot as if about
> to burst from their crusty shells;
> and like a child again
> marveled to hear so clear
> and brave a music pour

from such a small machine:
What makes the engine go?
Desire, desire, desire,
The longing for the dance
stirs in the buried life.
One season only,
and it's done.
So let the battered old willow
thrash against the windowpanes
and the house timbers creak.
Darling, to you remember
the man you married? Touch me,
remind me who I am.

Roger Housden wrote about this poem in his article "One Life, One Season," in an issue of *AARP.* Noting that the crickets are trilling their mating song, Housden writes, "It is late summer for Kunitz, too, and he is keenly aware that his last days are all too near. But does that mean he has nothing to do? Far from it. The marvelous thing in this poem is that Kunitz realizes his season lasts for the duration of his lifetime. The desire, the engine of his life, will continue until his dying breath. Knowing this, he is not afraid."[18]

Thus, here, we have the testimony of a very old man that desire never fails. To be sure, one may, as Kunitz says, have trouble from time to time recalling who he is. But that's another story, one that is beside the point. In fact, one could argue that as memory begins to totter a bit, desire becomes the more steady and firm. So invoking that great Protestant tradition that we listen to our preachers so that we can disagree with them—especially if they are younger than we are—I suggest that Ecclesiastes 12:5b be revised from "the grasshopper drags itself along and desire fails" to "the grasshopper drags itself along because desire never fails." The older, wiser Solomon would have wanted it this way. So let the battered old willow thrash against the windowpanes and the house timbers creak. Listen, instead, to the purring of the engine.

Implications for Ministers of Good Humor

What can we Ministers of Good Humor learn from the foregoing discussion of the aging process? Well, one of the things it teaches me is that a sense of humor is an integral part—but only a part—of a whole philosophy of aging. Such a philosophy includes continuing to grow and not allowing oneself to stagnate, energetic commitment to a daily routine, remaining actively involved with other people, and acting on one's need to be needed. When humor tries to carry the ball all by itself, it becomes strained, stressed-out, and sterile. It needs to be a team player, working with the other four members of the team to get the ball into the basket.

Another thing this discussion of the aging process teaches me is that *humor needs to be on the side of integrity over despair.* This means that it should not deny that there is a measure of despair in the experience of growing old. In fact, humor derives its vitality not from ignoring despair but by contributing to the ongoing task of maintaining an appropriate "ratio" of integrity over despair. To the list of four strategies for maintaining integrity over despair discussed above, I would add the strategy of humor, which would ideally include all four dimensions of humor identified by James Thorson and F. C. Powell in their multidimensional sense of humor scale (as discussed in chapter 1). These are coping humor, humor production, humor appreciation, and appreciation of humorous people.

A third thing that this discussion of the aging process teaches me is that if one is to have a sense of humor about oneself, *it should be on the side of self-forgiveness, not self-accusation or self-ridicule.* Freud's "Humor" article, published when he was seventy-one years old, surprised everyone because he suggested that humor is "located" in the part of our minds that reflects our sense of morality (or internalized "parental function," otherwise called the "super-ego"). He said that we know "the super-ego is a stern master," but it also has a kinder, gentler side, one that speaks "kindly words of comfort to the intimidated ego."[19] He concluded that not everyone is capable of this humorous attitude (probably because for them the stern master side of the "super-ego" will not allow it): "It is a rare and precious gift, and there are many people who have not even the capacity for deriving pleasure from humor when it is presented to them by others."[20]

Humor and Illness

I have already said that although I do not believe that laughter is the best medicine, humor is the best placebo. This belief is supported by the empirical evidence presented in chapter 1 that humor helps to moderate life-stress and to reduce anxiety and mild forms of depression. Because illness can have one or more of these effects, humor may not cure our bodily ills, but it can help us cope with them. There's the joke about the man who says to his doctor, "My back aches, I have chronic indigestion, my bowels are sluggish, and I don't feel so good myself." Humor won't remove the first three maladies, but it can do something for the fourth, and this can help him cope with the others. And this is where the placebo comes in.

Humor as Placebo

The Merck Manual of Medical Information informs us that placebos are substances that are made to resemble drugs but do not contain an active drug; instead they contain an inactive substance such as sugar or starch. Their name derives from the Latin word *placebo*, which means "I shall please." The word *placebo* first appeared in a medical dictionary in 1785 and was described as "a commonplace method of medicine." Two editions later, it was described as "a make-believe medicine," allegedly inert and harmless.[21] The *Manual* notes, however, that we now know that placebos can have both positive *and* negative effects:

Placebos can result in or be coincidentally associated with many changes, both desirable and undesirable. This phenomenon, called the placebo effect, appears to have two components: anticipation of results, usually optimistic, from taking a drug (sometimes called suggestibility);

and spontaneous change. Sometimes people improve spontaneously, without treatment. If spontaneous change—whether positive or negative—occurs after a placebo is taken, the placebo may incorrectly be credited with or blamed for the result.[22]

I may be a little dense, but I fail to see how anyone would know that the placebo *didn't* produce the positive spontaneous change. It's blaming the placebo for a negative spontaneous change that's incorrect, and unfair to the harmless little placebo. In any event, the *Manual* points out that:

> Some people seem more susceptible to the placebo effect than others. People who have a positive opinion of drugs, doctors, nurses, and hospitals are more likely to respond favorably to placebos than are people who have a negative opinion. Some people who are particularly susceptible to placebos tend to become compulsive about using the drug; they tend to increase the dose, and they develop withdrawal symptoms when they are deprived of the placebo.[23]

Placebos are used in studies of the effects of new drugs, and the drug must perform significantly better than the placebo to justify its use: "In some studies, as many as 50% of the participants taking the placebo improve (an example of the placebo effect), making it difficult to show the effectiveness of the drug being tested."[24]

Since I am suggesting that humor should not be credited with anything other than a "placebo effect," it would be interesting to know whether any studies have been conducted in which all the participants are given a placebo, but half are informed and the other half are not informed that it is a placebo. Does knowing that it is a placebo increase or decrease its "placebo effect"? As I know that humor is a placebo, do I receive greater *or* lesser benefits from humor than does a person, obviously dull-witted, who doesn't know this? But a more pressing issue that the *Manual* raises is the fact that one may become compulsive about using a placebo and require steadily increasingly doses, and may also experience withdrawal symptoms when deprived of the placebo. Does this apply to humor as well? On the basis of personal experience, I would advise every Minister of Good Humor to engage in some rather careful self-monitoring in this regard for, to the best of my knowledge, there is no twelve-step program available for the placebo addict. Finally, one would assume that the best placebo in cases of illness would be jokes that are, in fact, about illness. There are many, many jokes on this whole subject. In the interest of brevity, I suggest that we focus on doctor jokes.

"The Doctor Will See You Now"

The very title of this section recalls the joke about the nurse who tells the doctor that a man who claims to be invisible is sitting in the waiting room. The doctor replies, "Tell him I can't see him today." I will not dwell on the many doctor jokes that focus on what doctors charge, such as the following: As a doctor was examining his patient, he asked, "Any coughing, wheezing, or shortness of cash?" Instead, I want to consider jokes that concern the two issues that are most likely to make one anxious: (1) the diagnosis and (2) the treatment.

Diagnosis. In some jokes, a doctor tells the patient who has just had a physical exam that there are grounds for concern:

Upon completing the patient's annual physical, a doctor told him to get dressed. "I'm afraid your condition is quite a lot worse than last year. The best thing for you to do would be to give up liquor and smoking and all that rich food you've been eating at fancy restaurants. You should also stop seeing all those young women who keep you out until all hours." The patient thought for a moment. "What's the next best thing?"

This patient is obviously reluctant to make the sacrifices that the doctor recommends. The following patient takes the "bad news" with surprising equanimity:

Ever since he graduated from high school, Brian spent most of his waking hours lounging on the couch, watching sports programs, and drinking beer. One day, as he reached for a can, he tumbled off the sofa onto his head and had to be rushed to the hospital. After X rays were taken, the doctor went right to Brian's bedside. "I'm sorry, but I have some bad news for you, young man. Your X rays show that you've broken a vertebra in your neck. I'm afraid you'll never work again." "Thanks, Doc. Now what's the bad news?"

In the following joke, what the doctor thought was "good news" proves otherwise:

After his annual physical examination, the patient asked his doctor, "Tell me, how long am I going to live?" "Don't worry, the doctor replied, "You'll probably live to be eighty!" "But doctor, I *am* eighty." "See, what did I tell you?"

Here's a joke in which the patient misunderstands what the doctor is telling him about the likely cause of his illness: "I can't find a cause for your illness," the doctor said. "Frankly, I think it's due to drinking." "In that case," replied his patient, "I'll come back when you've sobered up." And here's one where the patient understands only too well:

"How did it go at the doctor's today, honey?" "Not good. The doctor told me I have to take the medication he gave me for the rest of my life." "What's so terrible about that?" "He only gave me four pills."

As a group, these jokes address most of the anxieties that patients experience in relation to the diagnosis and prognosis, anxieties relating to the question of what one has, whether the diagnosis is accurate, what appears to be the long-term prognosis, how one's current way of life will be affected, and so forth. The jokes make light of these anxieties, treating the matter as "the very thing to jest about!"[25]

Treatment. The anticipation of invasive surgery and post-operative concerns may also cause considerable anxiety, which we often try to reduce through worry (thinking of all the possible things that might go wrong.) Humor is another way to approach it. We especially want to have confidence that our bodies are in good, competent hands. Here's a joke that addresses this concern:

> After undergoing a long and complicated operation, a patient kept complaining about a bump on his head and a horrible headache. Since his surgery had been an intestinal one, the nurse couldn't understand why he would be complaining about an aching head. Fearing that perhaps he might be suffering from some form of postsurgery shock, she decided to ask the surgeon who performed the operation. "There's nothing to worry about, nurse," explained the surgeon. "He actually does have a bump on his head. Halfway through the operation we ran out of anesthetic."

A surgeon causing unnecessary discomfort is bad enough. Even worse is a surgical mistake that is irrevocable. There are many jokes that play on this concern. Here's a typical one:

> A doctor visited the patient on whom he had just performed surgery and said, "I have some good news and some bad news." "Give me the bad news first." "Well, unfortunately, we amputated the wrong leg." "That's bad, all right. So what's the good news?" "Your other leg won't have to be amputated after all."

On the other hand, jokes that compare the competence of surgeons with that of auto mechanics usually come out in support of surgeons (which may say something about the confidence we have in the folks who work on our automobiles). An oft-told joke is the one about a mechanic who points out to the heart surgeon that he removes the valves, grinds them, puts in new parts, and when the work is done, the car "purrs like a kitten." So if they both do the same work, why is the heart surgeon making so much more money? The surgeon replies, "Try doing your work with the engine running." And this one:

A proctologist decided to make a life change and become a mechanic. He signed up for evening classes at the local technical school, attended faithfully, and learned all he could. As the time for the practical exam approached, he carefully prepared for weeks and passed the exam with remarkable skill. His instructor gave him a score of 150 percent. Puzzled by his extraordinarily high score, he went to his instructor and said, "I really appreciate the high score you gave me, but I am wondering if there is some mistake." His instructor replied, "Not at all. During the exam you took the engine apart perfectly. That was worth 50%. You put it back together again perfectly, which was worth another 50%. The extra 50% I gave you because you did all of it through the muffler!"

Finally, for some patients, the youthfulness of the doctor is a cause for concern. The following joke is illustrative:

A young medical student brandishing a syringe approached a patient in bed. "Nothing to worry about," said the student, "just a little prick with a needle." "Yes, I know you are," said the patient, "but what are you going to do?"[26]

Implications for Good Humor Ministry

The patient in the last joke focused on the "just a little prick with a needle" phrase, and ignored the "Nothing to worry about" phrase. This gives us a useful clue to how humor may be helpful in cases of illness, invasive surgery, and the like. As we saw in chapter 1, William E. Kelly found that both worry and humor serve as coping mechanisms in anxious situations, especially those over which the outcomes are out of one's control. Illnesses certainly qualify as anxious situations in this sense. The worrier reduces anxiety by anticipating all the things that could possibly go wrong, while the humorist reduces anxiety by minimizing the importance of what may *in fact* go wrong. I would guess that among worriers, the true believers are unlikely to be helped by the sorts of jokes presented here, while among the humorists, those who are humorists to the core are so well-immunized that they don't need jokes. In effect, their whole life is one big joke. It's for those of us who fall in-between—the ambivalent ones—that jokes like those presented here may be especially helpful. We are the ones who want to believe the young student who says that there is nothing to worry about, and, for us, a well-timed bit of humor may tip the scales in favor of minimizing the importance of what may *in fact* go wrong.

Some years ago, I was more-or-less relaxing in a hospital bed waiting to be wheeled off for eye surgery. Another guy was brought into the room in a wheelchair. We shared our stories as to why we were there, then he feel asleep. After a bit, an orderly appeared and said to me, "You the foot?" I said, "No, he's the foot." As they wheeled him out for surgery, I thought about what might have happened if both of us had been asleep, and I had gotten wheeled off for foot surgery. The thought of this possibility was pretty amusing to me at the time, and I couldn't wait to tell the doctor when I arrived in the operation room. This was a case of unintentional humor helping me cope with the anxiety of undergoing surgery. If the orderly had told a joke to the two of us, it may or may not have had the same effect. But jokes like the ones presented here can be tucked away in our heads for those times when it is natural to be anxious about what is about to happen, or what the doctor knows and is about to tell us, and so forth. They won't cure us of what ails us, but they can make us feel that it isn't as bad or won't be as bad as our worst fears.

Humor and Death

In the late 1960s, Elisabeth Kübler-Ross, a psychiatrist, and Carl A. Nighswonger, a chaplain, conducted a study of terminally ill patients at the University of Chicago Hospital. Both developed models of the stages of dying based on their research. Kübler-Ross's model became enormously influential through her book *On Death and Dying*.[27] She proposed that terminally ill patients go through five stages, including denial and isolation, anger, bargaining, depression, and acceptance; she also proposed that hope might occur at any of these stages, but is more likely in the acceptance stage.

Nighswonger proposed a more dialectical model involving six stages, including denial vs. panic, catharsis vs. depression, bargaining vs. selling out, realistic hope vs. despair, acceptance vs. resignation, and fulfillment vs. forlornness.[28] His own untimely death prohibited him from completing his own book based on the interviews with terminally ill patients. Although the model derived from interviews with terminally ill patients, it came to be applied more to the grief process following the death of a loved one.

We may assume that the patients who were interviewed were experiencing *acute* death anxiety, and therefore the models track the stages in the acute death anxiety experience. An issue this raises for me is the *chronic* state of death anxiety that we all experience to greater or lesser degrees. Many persons say that they have no fear of death, and undoubtedly this is true. But fears concern specific and recognizable dangers, while anxiety is a more diffuse sense of foreboding. This would account for the fact that worry is a common response to anxiety. I would guess that few of us go through a single day without having a thought, however fleeting, that we or someone we love will die someday. We may not be obsessed with the thought, but few of us, I believe, are total strangers to a sort of chronic, low-grade death anxiety. And this, I would propose, is where humor has a therapeutic role to play. This is the more likely focus for the Ministry of Good Humor than acute states of death anxiety.

In *A Time to Laugh* I suggest that there are five categories of jokes (which we might think of as representing stages) relating to chronic death anxiety:[29] (1) how to react to being informed by a doctor that one is much closer to death than one had ever imagined; (2) how to manage the inevitable awkwardness of the deathbed scenario; (3) how to conduct ourselves at funerals; (4) how to wrap our minds around the unknown that follows death (Saint Peter and the Pearly Gates to the rescue)[30]; and (5) how to come to terms with the fact that some loved ones will outlive us or, expressed more gracefully, how they will manage when we are gone.[31] I provide several pages of jokes illustrating the stages of chronic death anxiety. My own favorites tend to be funeral jokes, which reflect the idea that because a funeral involves a death, it really ought to go awry. This was confirmed for me by the story a funeral director's daughter told me of the funeral of a husband who loved motorcycles, and his wife, who always rode with him. Immediately following the funeral service, his wife jumped on the casket for "one last ride."

This true story is almost as bad as the joke about the guy who punched the deceased on the nose, then explained to the other mourners, "Hey, he hit me first!" Or the guy who asked someone to take a snapshot of him shaking hands with the deceased. Or the one about the guy whose father dies and he tells the funeral director that he wants to give his dad the best send-off that money can buy. A couple of weeks after the funeral, he receives a bill for $15,000, which he gladly pays. The next month there's another bill for $85, which he also pays, and another for $85 the following month. Puzzled, he calls up the funeral director who explains, "Well, you said you wanted the very best for your dad, so I rented him a tux."

The Epitaph and Death Anxiety

But jokes are not the only form of humor enabling us to address our chronic death anxieties. Another is the epitaph, a necessarily short inscription on a gravestone, often in verse form. Here are a few of my favorites:[32]

> Here lie I, Martin Elginbrod,
> Have mercy on my soul, Lord God.
> As I on you, were I Lord God
> And you were Martin Elginbrod.

> Here lies the body
> Of Jonathan Blake.
> Stepped on the gas pedal
> Instead of the brake.

> In memory of Jane Brent
> Who kicked up her heels
> And away she went.

> Open wide ye heavenly gates
> That lead to the heavenly shore.

Our father suffered in passing through,
And mother weighs much more.

Who far below this tomb dost rest,
Has joined the army of the blest.
The Lord has taken her to the sky,
The saints rejoice and so do I.

Under this sod
And under these trees
Lieth the body of Solomon Pease.
He's not in this hole,
But only his pod;
He shelled out his soul
And went up to God.

Here lies the body of our Anna
Done to death by a banana.
It wasn't the fruit that laid her low
But the skin of the thing that made her go.

As our Dumb Blonde might say when death beckons, "Here we go again."

When I was a boy, I would accompany my grandfather on his cemetery walks. He would sit on a bench communing with his dead while I wandered around looking at the gravestones in search of epitaphs and other oddities. When others were keeping vigil as my wife's mother lay in a coma a few hours before her death, I wandered out of the hospital and into the nearby cemetery, in search of gravestone epitaphs. A meaningless exercise? I think, rather, that it was an expression of *integrity over despair*, which took the form of "a sense of comradeship with men and women of distant times and of different pursuits who have created orders and objects and sayings conveying human dignity and love."[33] And if I had stumbled upon a humorous epitaph on one of the gravestones, this would have reinforced my belief that the day will come when God will wipe every tear from our eyes (Rev. 21:3)—except, of course, our tears of laughter.

5

So You Want to Be a Minister of Good Humor?

A minister, a priest, and a rabbi go into a bar. The bartender says, "Hey, what is this, some kind of a joke?"

Throughout this handbook, I have been addressing the reader as one who has already enlisted in the Ministry of Good Humor. But now I need to "speak truth in love" (a religious euphemism for telling the other person what you really think of him or her). The truth is that reading a handbook on the Ministry of Good Humor is one thing, but putting it into practice is a whole different kettle of fish. And this raises the question, What makes a good candidate for ordination in the Ministry of Good Humor? Well, don't think this question hasn't occurred to the folks that head up our denomination. In fact, over the past couple of months, our research department (comprising a couple of fleet-footed angels wearing tennis shoes)[1] has been out observing experienced Ministers of Good Humor, and they have come back with the results.

The effective Minister of Good Humor has three traits or qualities: (1) is practical and down-to-earth; (2) is simple-minded; and (3) is comfortable with the person he or she already is. I could present you with the reams of data that our researchers compiled to arrive at this conclusion and describe the methodologies that they used (mostly, as you would have guessed yourself, questionnaires for acquiring the data, and factor-analysis for interpreting it). But I don't want to bore you with facts and figures. Instead, I will focus on the rabbi, who gets the best role in "minister, priest, and rabbi" jokes,[2] as the rabbi exemplifies the qualities that our researchers identified through their scientific research. I assume that the reader who has come this far with me does not need to be told that in lifting up the rabbi as an exemplar of the person who will make a good, effective Minister of Good Humor, I am not suggesting that the Christian churches should go out and drag real-life Jewish rabbis, kicking and screaming, into the Christian fold. Even as chapter 2 focused on a fictional bar and bartender, we're talking here about a fictional rabbi.

On the other hand, I would remind you of the account in the gospel of John of Jesus' appearance to Mary Magdalene in the garden after he had risen from the dead. At first she thought he was the gardener and called him "Sir" (a sign of her respect for gardeners, unless, of course, she had been taught survival tactics by a foul-mouthed parrot).[3] Aware of the coming American Burma-Shave jingle tradition, Jesus no doubt said, "Mary, O Mary, what's the trouble? Could it be my three day stubble?"[4] This query enabled her to catch on to who he really was, and she said to him in Hebrew, "Rabbouni!" (Jn. 20:16). For the benefit of the reader who doesn't know Hebrew from the proverbial hole in the ground, John adds parenthetically "(which means Teacher)." That Mary addressed Jesus in Hebrew seems a bit odd, since *Webster's New World College Dictionary* says that Aramaic was "a Northwest Semitic language that was the lingua franca throughout the Near East from c. 300 B. C. to c. A. D. 650; it replaced Hebrew as the language of the Jews, and one of its dialects was spoken by Jesus and his disciples."[4] Maybe John, in putting Hebrew words into Mary's mouth, was showing off his own knowledge of Hebrew.[5] But I digress. Let's get back to the jokes and the traits of the effective Minister of Good Humor.

Practical and Down-to-Earth

The effective Minister of Good Humor is practical and down-to-earth. *Webster's New World College Dictionary* has several definitions of the word *practical,* but the best ones for our purposes here are (1) concerned with the application of knowledge to useful ends, rather than with theory, speculation, etc.; and (2) concerned with, or dealing realistically and sensibly with everyday activities, work, etc. In comparing and contrasting *practical* with its synonym *practicable,* it says that *practical* "stresses effectiveness as tested by actual experience or as measured by a completely realistic approach to life or the particular circumstances involved."[6] "Down-to-earth" is another way of saying what *practical* says, as it means "realistic or practical," but it also suggests that the person is "without affectation" and "natural."[7] This means that the pompous ("characterized by exaggerated stateliness; pretentious, as in speech or manner; self-important") ass ("a stupid or silly person; a fool") need not apply.[8]

The practical and down-to-earth quality of the Minister of Good Humor is reflected in the following joke:

> A minister, a priest, and a rabbi die in a car crash. They go to heaven for orientation. They are all asked, "When you are in your casket, and friends, family, and congregants are mourning over you, what would you like to hear them say?" The minister says, "I would like to hear them say that I was a wonderful husband, a fine spiritual leader, and a great family man." The priest says, "I would like to hear that I was a wonderful teacher and a servant of God who made a huge difference in people's lives." The rabbi replies, "I would like to hear them say, 'Look, he's moving!'"

The rabbi here is both practical and down-to-earth. Where his colleagues want to hear meaningless plaudits (the usual bouquets that funeral speakers throw out to the rest of us, sitting glumly in the pews), the rabbi wants to hear something that is eminently practical and, for this reason, truly inspirational. Notice, too, that he wants it said by more than one individual, as it is important to him that the observation of this movement of the deceased is not one person's perverse idea of a joke. And, finally, the rabbi's reply is the very epitome of the "down-to-earth." Where the minister and the priest are content to be remembered by the friends, family, and congregants down below, the rabbi, quite literally, wants to get back down to earth, and knows that the only way this will happen is if they notice that he isn't dead yet.

Here's another illustration of the rabbi's practical nature and resistance to engaging in grandiose ideas:

A minister, a priest, and a rabbi were discussing the unforeseen possibility of sudden death. The minister said, "We will all die someday, and none of us really knows when, but if we *did* know, we would all do a better job of preparing ourselves for that inevitable event." This comment prompted the rabbi to reply, "What would you do if you knew you only had four weeks of life remaining before your death and Judgment Day?" The minister said, "I would go out into my community and preach the gospel to those who have not yet accepted the Lord into their lives." The rabbi then asked the priest what he would do, and the priest replied, "I would dedicate all of my remaining time to serving God, my family, my church, and my fellow man with a greater conviction." "That's wonderful," the minister replied. Then the minister and the priest asked the rabbi what he would do, and he said, "I would go to my mother-in-law's house for the four weeks." The minister and priest were puzzled by this answer and asked, "Why your mother-in-law's home?" The rabbi replied, "Because that would be the longest four weeks of my life!"

Here again, the rabbi is practical and down-to-earth. He doesn't think of the influence he might have in his community as the minister does, and he doesn't think of this as a time of service, as the priest does. He merely thinks of how he can make it seem as though his last four weeks are an eternity, of sorts, and he has a workable plan for achieving this objective. In fact, what he proposes to do is a perfect illustration of the practical, which, as we have seen, "stresses effectiveness as tested by actual experience or as measured by a completely realistic approach to life or the particular circumstances involved."[9] He knows his mother-in-law, so his plan meets the "actual experience" test, and he therefore knows what four weeks spent in her house would be like, so his plan also meets the criterion of a "completely realistic approach to life or the particular circumstances involved." Unlike the minister, who will be out trying to convert the folks who have resisted or ignored his message for as long as he has been a member of the community, and unlike the priest, who plans to serve God and everyone under the sun with even greater conviction for four exhausting weeks, the rabbi's plan is foolproof. And lest we should charge him with acting out of pure selfishness while his colleagues are the very model of altruism, let us not forget that the woman with whom he will spend his last days on earth will make it a living hell. And what could be more self-sacrificing than that?

The following joke has the rabbi taking a different approach:

> A minister, a priest, and a rabbi were taken hostage by some bank robbers. Hours later the FBI was still standing tough; they wouldn't give the bank robbers a getaway car and an airplane to an undisclosed destination. The bank robbers gathered the three hostages in a corner and informed them that things looked bad for them, so they were going to try to make a run for it. Meanwhile, they would have to shoot the hostages. But to show that they were really decent guys underneath, they granted each hostage one wish. "Please," said the minister, "for the last two months I've been working on my Easter sermon. What a waste to die now without having delivered it before an audience. I'll go happily if you let me recite my sermon. It's a half-hour, forty-five minutes tops." Figuring that they had some time, they promised to

grant him the wish. "Please," said the priest, "I was ordained before Vatican II and before I go, I would like to say the Mass in Latin. It takes about forty-five minutes." The bank robbers look at their watches a little nervously, but to them, a promise is a promise, so they agreed. They turned to the rabbi, who said: "Please, I beg of you, shoot me first!"

Here again the rabbi is thinking in very practical, down-to-earth terms, though this time he's not trying to prolong his time alive. Unlike the other two, there is nothing more he needs to prove in life, and, moreover, given the choice (which itself is quite uncommon), he would rather not die a painful death. Thus, his request is based on the fact that he has made a realistic appraisal of "the particular circumstances involved."

Finally, it is important to note that the rabbi's practicality extends to his avoidance of theological debates, which he knows from experience will only end in stalemate or a compromise that leaves everyone feeling unhappy, if not bitter:

A minister, a priest, and a rabbi were discussing when life begins. The priest said that life begins at conception, while the minister believed that life begins at birth. The rabbi said, "Life begins when the kids move out and the dog is dead!"

Who could possibly argue with that?

Simple-mindedness

A second quality of the effective Minister of Good Humor is simple-mindedness. This quality may need some explanation, because simple-mindedness is often confused with the lack of sense or reasoning ability, and with being easily misled or deceived.[10] But the research team (remember the fleet-footed angels wearing tennis shoes?) told us at the workshop they conducted on identifying the qualities that make for effective Ministers of Good Humor, that *simple*, as they are using the term, is the opposite of *complex, involved,* and *disingenuous*. It also implies that saying less is probably better than saying more. With this clarification, let's look at the following account of what happened when the threesome decided to play poker together:

> A minister, a priest, and rabbi were playing poker when the police raided the game. Turning to the minister, the lead police officer said, "Reverend Allsworthy, were you gambling?" Turning his eyes to heaven the minister whispered, "Lord, forgive me for what I am about to do." To the police officer he then said, "No, officer, I was not gambling." The officer then asked the priest, "Father Murphy, were you gambling?" The priest whispered a little prayer of contrition, then replied, "No, officer, I was not gambling." Turning to the rabbi, the officer again asked, "Rabbi Goldstein, were you gambling?" Shrugging his shoulders, the rabbi replied, "With whom?"

Obviously, the rabbi had the advantage of going last. But lest you say that this gave him an unfair advantage over his gambling partners, it would be more accurate to suggest that going third is itself illustrative of simple-mindedness. No doubt when the police officer looked at the trio, he could see that the minister, in spite of what he was about to do, gave the impression of wanting to go first. Similarly, the priest probably gave the impression that he wanted to go second, especially since he planned to reinforce what the minister had said.

At any rate, the fact that both of them felt the need to say one thing to God and another to the police officer is concrete evidence of the complexity of their situation. If we had been there, we would have noticed their body language, the difficulty they were having meeting the police officer's gaze, their sweaty palms, etc. Compare the utter simplicity of the rabbi's comment—"With whom?"—and the shrug of his shoulders. Notice, too, that he responds to the police officer's question with a question of his own, thus tossing the ball back into the questioner's court. He is no simpleton, devoid of reasoning powers, and he is not one who is easily misled or deceived. Nor does he underestimate the police officer, assuming that *he* is a simpleton and easily misled and deceived. Most importantly, he does not perjure himself, and because he doesn't, he does not owe God an apology or confession.

Another illustration of the rabbi's simple-mindedness is the following story of the threesome out on the walk together:

> A minister, a priest, and a rabbi went for a hike one day. It was very hot. They were sweating and exhausted when they came upon a small lake. Since it seemed fairly secluded, they took off all their clothes and jumped in the water. Feeling refreshed, the trio decided to pick a few berries while enjoying their freedom. As they were crossing an open area, who should come along but a group of ladies from town. Unable to get to their clothes in time, the minister and the priest covered their privates and the rabbi covered his face while they ran for cover. After the ladies had left and the men got their clothes back on, the minister and the priest asked the rabbi why he had covered his face rather than his privates. The rabbi replied, "I don't know about you, but in my congregation, it's my face they would recognize."

At first glance the rabbi's instinctive reaction to the ladies' appearance may recall how small children cover their faces when they are embarrassed. But his explanation to the others indicates that the minister and priest acted from embarrassment. In contrast, his response was strategic and deceptively simple. Also, there's a note of moral self-confidence in the phrase, "I don't know about you," which suggests the possibility that one or more of the ladies *might* recognize the privates of the other clergymen. And this brings us to the third quality of effective Ministers of Good Humor, the feeling of being comfortable with who one is.

Comfortable With Who One Is

The third quality of the effective Minister of Good Humor is being comfortable with who one is. The word *comfortable* was suggested to me by the joke about the rabbi who was knocked down by a car. The paramedic loaded him on a stretcher and asked, "Are you comfortable?" The rabbi replied, "I make a good living." *Webster's New World College Dictionary* defines *comfortable* in the paramedic's sense as "in a state of comfort, at ease in body or mind; contented," and in the rabbi's sense as "sufficient to satisfy, adequate (a *comfortable* salary)."[11] In considering synonyms of the word, *Webster's* says that *comfortable* "implies the absence of disturbing, painful, or distressing features and, in a positive sense, stresses ease, contentment, and freedom from care." The words *at ease* and *contentment* loom large in these various definitions, and this is precisely what the researchers picked up from the questionnaires they passed out to the individuals—both lay and clergy—who were engaged in the Ministry of Good Humor: these ministers were "at ease" and "content" with who they are.

Here's a minister, priest, and rabbi joke that illustrates the rabbi's comfort with who he is:

> A minister, a priest, and a rabbi were all stuck on a God-forsaken island for a number of years. One day they found a magic lamp! They rubbed it, and a genie came out and said that because there were three of them, they each would get one wish. The minister was quick to respond, "After all these years on this miserable island, I want to go back to my church and my manse in Louisville." *Poof!*, he disappears. The priest said, "I agree wholeheartedly with the minister. This is a miserable place, and I can't wait to leave, but send me to my church and my rectory in Boston." *Poof!*, he too disappears. The rabbi's turn was next. He said, "I can certainly understand how they feel about this island, but I sort of like it and I just wish my two buddies were back." *Poof!!*

This joke suggests that, considering everything, the rabbi isn't convinced that going back to where he came from would be an improvement on what he has had the last several years. It also indicates that he has developed an affection for the minister and the priest, and has come to value their companionship. We could read into the joke some other possible meanings, such as that he knows that the minister and priest will not find any greater happiness in Louisville and Boston than they have experienced on this God-forsaken island, so he feels that he is doing them a favor by arranging for their return. But we could just as well suggest that he knows what he himself needs to remain comfortable with himself, and what he needs is to have his two buddies back.

Then there's the joke about the two men who come to the rabbi's study to settle a dispute:

> The first man explained his side of the story, and argued his case with great eloquence. After a moment's reflection, the rabbi said to him, "You're right." Then the other man presented his side, and he was equally eloquent. After a moment's reflection, the rabbi said to him, "You're right." After the two men left, the rabbi's wife was upset, and she said to her husband, "They have conflicting stories. How could you say that both of them were right? One is right, and the other is wrong. You can't have it both ways." The rabbi thought long and hard and finally said to his wife, "You know, you're right."

The rabbi in this joke is so comfortable with who he is that he can agree with his wife's observation that what he said to the two men couldn't possibly be right. At best, it was half-right and half-wrong, and where does that get you? A person who was not at ease with himself would almost certainly have gotten defensive when his wife told him that he really had blown it. He offers no defense, no rationalization, no explanation. So in the end, he has declared that everyone is right. And what's wrong with that?

So if you are practical and down-to-earth, if you are simple-minded, and if you are comfortable with yourself as you are, our denominational headquarters wants to hear from you. You should receive a postcard in the mail—snail mail, of course—acknowledging your ordination and instructing you to begin your ministry without delay. Speaking of snails, slow me down if you have heard this one:

A turtle was mugged and robbed by a gang of snails. When the police asked for a description of the villains, the turtle replied, "I'm sorry, but I just don't know. It all happened so fast."

Notes

Preface

[1]Michael Agnes, ed., *Webster's New World College Dictionary* (Foster City, Calif.: IDG Books Worldwide, 2001), 644.

[2]Ibid., 918.

[3]Ibid., 917.

[4]Ibid., 611.

[5]Ibid., 611.

[6]Ibid., 696.

[7]Ibid., 574.

[8]Ibid., 919.

[9]Author unknown. In Sarah Anne Stuart, comp. *A Treasury of Poems: A Collection of the World's Most Famous and Familiar Verse* (New York: Galahad Books, 1996), 527–28.

[10]I.J. Bartlett, "The Town of Don't You Worry," in *The Best Loved Poems of the American People*, comp. Hazel Felleman (Garden City, New York: Doubleday and Company, 1936), 103.

Chapter 1: What Good Is Humor?

[1]Robert R. Provine, *Laughter: A Scientific Investigation* (New York: Penguin Books, 2000), 189–207.

[2]Norman Cousins, *The Anatomy of an Illness as Perceived by the Patient* (New York: W. W. Norton and Company, 1979). *Ankylosing spondylitis* is inflammation of the spine and large joints, resulting in stiffness and pain. Mild to moderate flare-ups of inflammation generally alternate with periods of almost no symptoms. The most common symptom is back pain, which varies in intensity from one episode to another and one person to another. Pain in the lower back and the associated muscle spasms are often relieved by bending forward. Therefore, people often assume a stooped posture, which can lead to a permanent bent-over position. Most people develop some disabilities but can still lead normal, productive lives. In some people, the disease is more progressive, causing severe deformities. The long-range goals of treatment are to maintain proper posture and develop strong back muscles. Mark H. Beers, ed., *The Merck Manual of Medical Information*, 2d ed. (New York: Pocket Books, 2003), 377.

[3]Provine, 195.

[4]Study cited in ibid., 198.

[5]Ibid., 199.

[6]Edward Shorter, *From Paralysis to Fatigue: A History of Psychosomatic Illness in the Modern Era* (New York: The Free Press, 1992).

[7]The following discussion is based on Herbert M. Lefcourt and Rod A. Martin, *Humor and Life Stress: Antidote to Adversity* (New York: Springer Publishing Company, 1986).

[8]Ibid., 122.

[9]Smadar Bizi, Giora Keinan, and Benjamin Beit-Hallahmi, "Humor and Coping with Stress: A Test Under Real-Life Conditions," *Personality and Individual Differences*, vol. 9 (1988): 951–56.

[10]American Psychiatric Association, *The Diagnostic and Statistical Manual of Mental Disorders-DSM-IV* (Washington, D. C.: American Psychiatric Association, 1994), 341.

[11]Ibid., 349.

[12]Albert Porterfield, "Does Sense of Humor Moderate the Impact of Life Stress on Psychological and Physical Well-Being?," *Journal of Research in Personality* 21 (1987): 307–17.

[13]Stephanie L. Deaner and Jasmin T. McConatha, "The Relation of Humor to Depression and Personality," *Psychological Reports* 72 (1993): 755–63.

[14]Arthur M. Nezu, Christine M. Nezu, and Sonia E. Blissett, "Sense of Humor as a Moderator of the Relation Between Stressful Events and Psychological *Distress*: A Perspective Analysis," *Journal of Personality and Social Psychology* 54 (1988): 520–25.

[15]Michael Agnes, ed., *Webster's New World College Dictionary* (Foster City, Calif.: IDG Books Worldwide, 2001), 64.

[16]Aaron T. Beck and Gary Emery, *Anxiety Disorders and Phobias: A Cognitive Perspective* (New York: Basic Books, 1985), 67–81.

[17]*Ibid.*, 33.

[18]Ronald E. Smith, James C. Ascough, Ronald F. Ettinger, and Don A. Nelson, "Humor, Anxiety, and Task Performance," *Journal of Personality and Social Psychology* 19 (1971): 243–46.

[19]Nancy A. Yovetich, J. Alexander Dale, and Mary A. Hudek, "Benefits of Humor in Reduction of Threat-induced Anxiety," *Psychological Reports* 66 (1990): 51–58.

[20]James A. Thorson and F. C. Powell, "Relationships of Death Anxiety and Sense of Humor," *Psychological Reports* 72 (1993): 1364–66.

[21]William E. Kelly, "An Investigation of Worry and Sense of Humor," *The Journal of Psychology* 136 (2002): 657–66.

[22]Agnes, *Webster's New World College Dictionary*, 1651.

[23]Ibid., 662.

[24]Ibid., 663.

[24]Ibid.

[25]Ibid.

[26]Julie K. Norem, *The Positive Power of Negative Thinking* (New York: Basic Books, 2001).

[27]Billy Collins, "The Life of Riley: A Definitive Biography," in *Questions About Angels: Poems* (Pittsburgh: University of Pittsburgh Press, 1999), 67.

[28]The phrase "life of Riley" was popularized in a 1919 song with the lines, "Faith and my name is Kelly, Michael Kelly, but I'm living the life of Reiley just the same."

[29]Provine, *Laughter*, 27–28.

[30]Ibid., 28.

[31]Millicent Abel, "Interaction of Humor and Gender in Moderating Relationships Between Stress and Outcomes," *The Journal of Psychology* 132 (1998): 267–76.

[32]Ibid., 274.

[33]Donald Capps, *A Time to Laugh: The Religion of Humor* (New York: Continuum Press, 2005), 69–76.

[34]Marc Gelkopf, Shulamith Kreitler, and Mircea Sigel, "Laughter in a Psychiatric Ward: Somatic, Emotional, Social, and Clinical Effects on Schizophrenic Patients," *The Journal of Nervous and Mental Disease* 181 (1993): 283–89.

[35]Ibid., 288.

[36]Ibid.

[37]Ibid.

[38]Welko Tomic, David M. Tomic, and Will E. G. Evers, "A Question of Burnout Among Reformed Church Ministers in the Netherlands," *Mental Health, Religion and Culture* 7: 225–47.

Chapter 2: Creating a Good Humor Ministry Ethos

[1]Michael Agnes, ed., *Webster's New World College Dictionary* (Foster City, Calif.: IDG Books Worldwide, 2001), 489.

[2]Albert Tapper and Peter Press, *A Guy Goes into a Bar...* (New York: MJF Books, 2000).

[3]Prohibition serves as an illustration in Paul Watzlawick, John Weakland and Richard Fisch's discussion of "when the solution becomes the problem" in their book, *Change: Principles of Problem Formation and Problem Resolution* (New York: W. W. Norton and Company, 1974), 31–32. They mention the corruptibility of the special police force recruited to enforce prohibition, smuggling, gangland warfare, the new public health problem created by the inferior quality of bootleg liquor, and the fact that the alcoholism rate actually increased!

[4]Michael R. Turner, ed., *Victorian Parlour Poetry: An Annotated Anthology* (New York: Dover Publications, Inc., 1967), 14–15.

[5]Ibid., 15–16.

[6]Agnes, *Webster's New World College Dictionary*, 91.

[7]Donald Capps, *Social Phobia: Alleviating Anxiety in an Age of Self-Promotion* (St. Louis: Chalice Press, 1998).

[8]Erik H. Erikson, "The Ontogeny of Ritualization in Man," in Erik H. Erikson, *A Way of Looking at Things: Selected Papers from 1930 to 1980*, ed. Stephen Schlein (New York: W. W. Norton and Company, 1987), 575–94; and Erik H. Erikson, *Toys and Reasons: Stages in the Ritualization of Experience* (New York: W. W. Norton and Company, 1977), 85–90.

[9]Agnes, *Webster's New World College Dictionary*, 436.

[10]David Riesman, with Reuel Denney and Nathan Glazer, *The Lonely Crowd: A Study of the Changing American Character* (New Haven: Yale University Press, 1950).

[11]Ibid., 15–16.

[12]Ibid., 21–22.

[13]Ibid., 25.

[14]John Bunyan, *The Pilgrim's Progress* (New York: Washington Square Press, 1957). Bunyan began writing *The Pilgrim's Progress* when he was in jail in 1675. The first part, focusing on Christian, was published in 1678. The second part, which focuses on Christian's family, was published in 1684. In my book *Deadly Sins and Saving Virtues* (Eugene, Oregon: Wipf and Stock Publishers, 2000), I relate Christian's journey to the life-cycle model formulated by Erik H. Erikson in *Childhood and Society*, rev. ed. (New York: W. W. Norton and Company, 1963), 247–74.

[15]Riesman, *The Lonely Crowd*, 26.

[16]David Riesman, with Nathan Glazer, *Faces in the Crowd: Individual Studies in Character and Politics*, abridged edition (New Haven: Yale University Press, 1965), 6.

[17]Ibid., 6.

[18]Riesman, *The Lonely Crowd*, 11–12.

[19]Ibid., 31–33.

[20]James Weldon Johnson, *God's Trombones: Seven Negro Sermons in Verse* (New York: Penguin Books, 1990), 17–20. Originally published in 1927.

[21]Henri J.M. Nouwen, *The Wounded Healer: Ministry in Contemporary Society* (New York: Image Books, 1979).

[22]Ibid., 83.

[23]Ibid.

[24]Ibid.

[25]Ibid., 85.

[26]Ibid., 89.

[27]Stephen Dunn, "Collecting Future Lives," *Between Angels* (New York: W. W. Norton and Company, 1989), 99–100.

[28]Agnes, ed., *Webster's New World College Dictionary*, 1450.

[29]William Stafford, "Scars," *An Oregon Message* (New York: Harper and Row, 1987), 41.

[30]William Glasser, *Reality Therapy: A New Approach to Psychiatry* (New York: Harper and Row, 1965), 22.

[31]Ibid., 22.

[32]Webster's New World College Dictionary, 1621.

[33]Donald Capps, *Reframing: A New Method in Pastoral Care* (Minneapolis: Fortress Press, 1990), 28–30.

[34]Ibid., 30. Slightly modified from original.

Chapter 3: Good Humor Role Models

[1]Sigmund Freud, as quoted in Elliott Oring, *The Jokes of Sigmund Freud: A Study in Humor and Jewish Identity* (Philadelphia: University of Pennsylvania Press, 1984), 16.

[2]Ibid., 16.

[3]Oring, *The Jokes of Sigmund Freud*, 17–18.

[4]Peter Gay, *Freud: A Life for Our Time* (New York: W. W. Norton and Company, 1988), 8.

[5]Ibid., 55.

[6]Sigmund Freud, *The Interpretation of Dreams*, trans. James Strachey (New York: Avon Books, 1965). Originally published in 1900.

[7]Sigmund Freud, *The Psychopathology of Everyday Life: Forgetting, Slips of the Tongue, Bungled Actions, Superstitutions, and Errors*, trans. James Strachey (New York: W. W. Norton and Company, 1960). Originally published in 1901.

[8]Sigmund Freud, *Jokes and Their Relation to the Unconscious*, trans. James Strachey (New York: W. W. Norton and Company, 1960). Originally published in 1905.

[9]Sigmund Freud, *An Autobiographical Study*, trans. James Strachey (New York: W. W. Norton and Company, 1952), 124. Originally published in 1925.

[10]Freud, *Jokes and Their Relation to the Unconscious*, 293.

[11]Sigmund Freud, "Thoughts for the Times on War and Death," in Sigmund Freud, *On Creativity and the Unconscious: Papers on the Psychology of Art, Literature, Love, Religion*, ed. Benjamin Nelson, reprint ed. (New York: Harper & Row, 1958).

[12]Ibid., 217.

[13]Sigmund Freud, "Humor," reprinted in Sigmund Freud, *Character and Culture*, ed. Philip Rieff (New York: Collier Books, 1963), 263.

[14]In Erik Erikson, *Young Man Luther: A Study in Psychoanalysis and History* (New York: W. W. Norton and Company, 1958). Erikson uses Freud's "economic" theory to talk about Martin Luther's distinction between "works" which are done for extrinsic reward and "work" which is intrinsically meaningful, being the expression of faith. He writes, "Many individuals should not do the work which they are doing, if they are doing it well at *too great inner expense*. Good work it may be in terms of efficiency; but it is also bad works," 220 (emphasis added).

[15]Freud, "Humor," 266.

[16]Theodor Reik, *Jewish Wit* (New York: Gamut Press, 1962), 75.

[17]Freud, *Jokes and Their Relation to the Unconscious*, 63–64.

[18]Ibid., 64.

[19]Ibid., 134.

[20]Ibid., 135.

[21]Ibid.

[22]Ibid.

[23]Ibid.

[24]Reik, *Jewish Wit*, 76. The same punch line occurs in a joke in Alan King's *Great Jewish Joke Book* (New York: Crown Publishers, 2002), but the beggar has been downgraded to a "bum," and the rich man is now a "Jewish mother," 99. In

this version, there are no remaining vestiges of what Freud calls the "religious" viewpoint (the sacred duty of charity of a Jewish person of means to a Jewish person who is poor).

[25]Freud, *Jokes and Their Relation to the Unconscious*, 135.

[26]Freud, "Humor," 268.

[27]Oring, *The Jokes of Sigmund Freud*, 17–18.

[28]Freud, *Jokes and Their Relation to the Unconscious*, 71. Slightly reworded.

[29]Ibid., 71.

[30]Ibid.

[31]Ibid., 72. Slightly reworded.

[32]Ibid.

[33]Ibid., 74–75. Slightly reworded.

[34]Ibid., 75.

[35]Ibid., 128.

[36]Ibid.

[37]Ibid., 75. Slightly reworded.

[38]Ibid., 75–76.

[39]Ibid., 127.

[40]Ibid.

[41]Ibid.

[42]Ibid., 293.

[43]Michael Agnes, ed., *Webster's New World College Dictionary* (Foster City, Calif.: IDG Books Worldwide, 2001), 1242.

[44]Martha Lupton, ed., *The Treasury of Modern Humor* (Indianapolis: Maxwell Droke, Publisher, 1938).

[45]*Best Lawyer Jokes Ever* (New York: Sterling Publishing Company, 2003).

[46]Michael Billig, *Freudian Repression: Conversation Creating the Unconscious* (Cambridge: Cambridge University Press, 1999).

[47]Rodney Rothman, *Early Bird: A Memoir of Premature Retirement* (New York: Simon and Shuster, 2005).

[48]James V. O'Connor, *Cuss Control: The Complete Book on How to Curb Your Cursing* (New York: Three Rivers Press, 2000), 13. In support of my use of the foul-mouthed parrot here, O'Connor cites the case of a woman who began to swear when she became a reporter for a major city newspaper, who reported on herself: "I didn't consciously start to swear. I just picked it up like a parrot," p. 41. For readers interested in the history of human cussing, I strongly recommend Geoffrey Hughes' *Swearing: A Social History of Foul Language, Oaths and Profanity in English* (London: Penguin Books, 1998). Given the quality of his scholarship, Hughes richly deserves appointment as Regius Professor of History at the Cuss Control Academy.

[49]O'Connor, 14. O'Connor has an account of a seventeen-year-old boy who got a job as Barney the Dinosaur for a promotion in a shopping mall. The first day on the job, some moms with preschoolers came in, and the kids were all over him. He panicked and tried to run away, but the kids chased him and he fell. A kid then jumped on his big Barney head and knocked it off, which prompted him to swear at the kid: "Get the —— off." He recalls remorsefully, "I laugh about it now, but I felt terrible. It was such a simple job, and I blew it after five minutes," p. 53.

[50]Bob Phillips, *The Best Ever Book of Good Clean Jokes* (Edison, New Jersey: Galahad Books, 1998).

[51]Christie Davies, *Jokes and Their Relation to Society* (Berlin: Mouton de Gruyter, 1998), 11.

[52]Ibid., 65–69.

[53]Susan Nolen-Hoeksema, *Women Who Think Too Much: How to Break Free of Over-thinking and Reclaim Your Life* (New York: Henry Holt and Company, 2003).

[54]Ibid., 14.

[55]Ibid., 11–12, 16.

[56]Sean Kelly and Rosemary Rogers, *Saints Preserve Us! Everything You Need to Know About Every Saint You'll Ever Need* (New York: Random House, 1993). They

include five saints who devote their time, in whole or in part, to lawyers. My favorite is Saint Ivo of Kermartin, a thirteenth century lawyer who was the subject of a French nursery rhyme: "Saint Ivo was a lawyer, and a Breton as well / But not a liar, strange to tell," 145–46. He was an advocate for the poor and oppressed, and especially concerned for orphans. Perhaps he was in the courtroom the day our heartless lawyer appealed to the jury to show mercy toward a client who had murdered his parents.

[57]Peter Abelard, *Historia Calamitatum: The Story of My Misfortunes: An Autobiography*, trans. Henry Adams Bellows (Saint Paul, Minn.: Thomas A Boyd, 1922). Cited in Donald Capps and Walter H. Capps, eds., *The Religious Personality* (Belmont, Calif.: Wadsworth Publishing Company, 1970), 113.

[58]The "iron cage" is Max Weber's term for modern rational society. He especially draw attention to its bureaucratic aspects. In *Jokes and Their Relation to Society*, cited earlier, Christie Davies suggests that stupidity jokes that project stupid traits onto other groups "serve to dispel our anxiety that we too may become completely absorbed into a competitive and bureaucratic world. The conforming message of the jokes is that it is the others who are irrationally rational whilst we are wise enough not to be trapped in the constricting formal and technical rationality of the iron cage," 77.

Chapter 4: Aging, Illness, and Death

[1]Robert R. Provine, *Laughter: A Scientific Investigation* (New York: Penguin Books, 2000), 187.

[2]Erik H. Erikson, *Childhood and Society* (New York: W. W. Norton and Company, 1950), 219–34. Some of the words have been changed over the years, but in the last book he wrote, *The Life Cycle Completed: A Review* (New York: W. W. Norton & Company, 1982), the stages are described as follows: *Infancy:* Basic Trust vs. Basic Mistrust; *Early Childhood:* Autonomy vs. Shame and Doubt; *Play Age:* Initiative vs. Guilt; *School Age:* Industry vs. Inferiority; *Adolescence:* Identity vs. Identity Confusion; *Young Adulthood*: Intimacy vs. Isolation; *Adulthood:* Generativity vs. Stagnation; *Old Age*: Integrity vs. Despair and Disgust. In the extended version of *The Life Cycle Completed* (New York: W. W. Norton and Company, 1997) published after his death, his wife, Joan M. Erikson, adds a chapter of her own that proposes a ninth stage, in which the words remain the same, but they are reversed. I have suggested a relocation of the stages according to decades, with two additional stages—Release vs. Control and Desire vs. Struggle—in one's 80s and 90s. See Donald Capps, *The Decades of Life* (Louisville: Westminster John Knox Press, forthcoming).

[3]Erik H. Erikson, Joan M. Erikson, and Helen Q. Kivnick, *Vital Involvement in Old Age: The Experience of Old Age in Our Time* (New York: W. W. Norton and Company, 1986).

[4]Erik H. Erikson, "Human Strength and the Cycle of Generations," *Insight and Responsibility* (New York: W. W. Norton and Company, 1964), 109-57.

[5]Ibid., 133–34.

[6]Ben Furman and Tapani Ahola, *Solution Talk: Hosting Therapeutic Conversations* (New York: W. W. Norton and Company, 1992), 18.

[7]Ibid., 23. In "The 'Midrash' and Biographic Rehabilitation," Mordechai Rotenberg discusses how Joseph revised the meaning of his experience of being sold into slavery by telling his brothers that God meant this for good, so that the lives of many people would be saved: So "do not be distressed, or angry with yourselves, because you sold me here; for God sent me before you to preserve life" (Gen. 45:5). Rotenberg calls this "re-biography of the sinful past," and notes that if a person was truly repentant, such revision of the past was considered legitimate by the Talmudic Sages. *Journal for the Scientific Study of Religion* 25 (1986): 41–53.

[8]Just as the Dumb Blonde jokes in chapter 3 raise the question of misogyny, so jokes about older persons raise the question of ageism. I want readers to know

that I am aware of these and related concerns, such as ethnicity (for example, the Murphy twins joke in chapter 2), and that I have addressed them in *A Time to Laugh: The Religion of Humor* (New York: Continuum Press, 2005), 69–76. For an excellent article on ageism, see Jeff Greenberg, Jeff Schimel, and Andy Martens, "Ageism: Denying the Face of the Future," in Todd D. Nelson, ed., *Ageism: Stereotyping and Prejudice Against Older Persons* (Cambridge, Mass.: MIT Press, 2004), 27–48.

[9]Greenberg, Schimel, and Martens, *Ibid.,* note that the two major stereotypes of older persons are that they are bad drivers and favor reducing taxes at the expense of education. The three most common forms of discrimination are in hiring, forced retirement, and negative depictions in mass media.

[10]I suggested in *A Time to Laugh* that certain issues in older person jokes, such as their ability to produce children at an advanced age, are projections onto older persons of the sexual anxieties of adolescents and young adults (80–84).

[11]Michael Agnes, ed., *Webster's New World College Dictionary* (Foster City, Calif.: IDG Books Worldwide, 2001), 391.

[12]James Ball Naylor, "Authorship," in Russell Baker, ed. *The Norton Book of Light Verse* (New York: W. W. Norton and Company, 1986), 164.

[13]Leland Ryken, *Words of Delight: A Literary Introduction of the Bible,* 2nd ed. (Grand Rapids, Mich..: Baker Book House, 1992).

[14]Ibid., 326–28.

[15]Louise Gluck, *The Wild Iris* (Hopewell, New Jersey: The Ecco Press, 1992), 43.

[16]Agnes, *Webster's New World College Dictionary,* 1545.

[17]Stanley Kunitz, "Touch Me," from *The Collected Poems* (New York: W. W. Norton and Company, 2000), 266. Kunitz died in 2006 at the age of 100. His last book, *The Wild Braid: A Poet Reflects on a Century in the Garden* (New York: W. W. Norton and Company, 2005), written with the assistance of Genine Lentine, has an account of a health crisis in the Spring of 2003 when he believed himself to be dying. He refers to this three-day crisis as a period "when I was in the other world" (118).

[18]Roger Housden, "One Life, One Season," *AARP* (July-August, 2003), 37.

[19]Sigmund Freud, "Humor," in Sigmund Freud, *Character and Culture,* ed. Philip Rieff (New York: Collier Books, 1963), 268.

[20]Ibid., 268–69.

[21]Mark H. Beers, ed., *The Merck Manual of Medical Information,* 2nd home edition (New York: Pocket Books, 2003), 61. Interestingly enough, *Webster's New World College Dictionary, Ibid.,* uses the word "humor" in its definition of placebo: "A harmless, unmedicated preparation given as a medicine to a patient *merely to humor him,* or used as a control in testing the efficacy of another medicated substance," 1099 (emphasis added).

[22]Ibid., 61.

[23]Ibid.

[24]Ibid.

[25]Freud, "Humor," 268.

[26]This joke does not belong in a respectable handbook for Ministers of Good Humor, but a foul-mouthed parrot who was retiring to Florida asked me to pass it along, and I foolishly promised him I would. About his retirement: A guy goes into a bar where a horse behind the bar is serving drinks. The guy is staring at the horse when the horse says, "Hey, buddy. What are you staring at? Haven't you ever seen a horse serving drinks before?" The guy says, "No, it's not that. It's just that I never thought the parrot would sell the place."

[27]Elisabeth Kübler-Ross, *On Death and Dying* (New York: Macmillan Company, 1969).

[28]Carl A. Nighswonger, "Ministry to the Dying as a Learning Encounter," *Journal of Thanatology* 1 (1971: 101–8.

[29]Donald Capps, *A Time to Laugh: The Religion of Humor* (New York: Continuum Press, 2005), 24. My "Nervous Laughter: Lament, Death Anxiety, and Humor,"

compares this model with the lament form in biblical psalms. In Sally A. Brown and Patrick D. Miller, eds., *Lament: Reclaiming Practices in Pulpit, Pew, and Public Square* (Louisville: Westminster John Knox Press, 2005), 70–79.

[30]My poem celebrating the career of S. S. Adams, inventor of sneezing powder and distributor of the joy buzzer appears in my article, "The Melancholy Boy and the Religion of Humor: The Case of S. S. Adams," Forthcoming in *Pastoral Psychology* (2008). It concludes with this reference to his final repose: "There he lies in grand estate, / The prankster potentate, / With buzzer primed to shake the hand, / Of Peter at the Gate."

[31]Men have greater reason to experience this anxiety stage because women tend to live longer (on average, 7 years). If you are curious as to why this is, and what men should do about it, you will want to read Donald Capps and Nathan Carlin, "Methuselah and Company: A Case of Male Envy of Female Longevity," forthcoming in Pastoral Psychology (2008).

[32]My source for these epitaphs is The Mammoth Book of Jokes, ed. Geoff Tibballs (New York: Carroll & Graf 2000), 367–84.

[33]Erik H. Erikson, *Identity: Youth and Crisis* (New York: W. W. Norton and Company, 1968), 139.

Chapter 5: So You Want to Be a Minister of Good Humor?

[1]You have every right to ask what qualifications these angels have for such an important task? The answer is simple: They were themselves subjects in a scientific experiment carried out by David Lester, as reported in his article, "The Learning of a Simple Maze Habit by Angels," published in *The Best of the Journal of Irreproducible Results*, ed. George H. Scherr (New York: Workman Publishing Company, 1983). He was able to acquire 30 Cherubim and 30 Archangels from the Carolina Theological Supply Company, so the problem of finding subjects for study was not as difficult as I would have thought. On the other hand, he reports: "The results of the study were unusual and many data had to be discarded." Only 5 subjects, all Archangels, successfully negotiated the "T" maze. 10 of the angels disappeared when placed in the start box, 24 walked outside of the maze, apparently passing through its walls. In the case of 10 angels, the reward disappeared while the angel was still in the start box, leading one of Lester's associates to hypothesize that, even as angels are not confined by space, neither are they confined by time. During the running of the 11 remaining angels, the experimenter had visions and was temporarily unable to continue with the study, an indication that scientific research may produce religious experiences, and which should prompt those who think that religion and science are incompatible to rethink their position. The angels who successfully negotiated the maze did so in one trial, leading Lester to conclude that angels' knowledge is intuitive. This is why Ministers of Good Humor should place their trust in science *and* angels.

[2]The lion's share of the jokes in this chapter are from Albert Tapper and Peter Press, *A Minister, a Priest, and a Rabbi* (Kansas City: Andrews McMeel Publishing, 2000).

[3]According to Sean Kelly and Rosemary Rogers' *Saints Preserve Us: Everything You Need to Know About Every Saint You'll Need* (New York: Random House, 1993), four saints devote full or part time to protecting gardeners: Dorothy, Rose of Lima, Rose of Viterbo, and Theresa of Lisieux, known as "The Little Flower." In contrast, there is only one patron saint of grave-diggers, Anthony the Great, who was probably given this grave responsibility because he spent 20 of his 105 years living in a tomb.

[4]My *A Time to Laugh: The Religion of Humor* (New York: Continuum Press, 2005) includes a number of biblical Burma Shave jingles under the general heading, "Motoring through the Bible Belt." Frank Rowsome, Jr. 's history of Burma-Shave signs in *The Verse By the Side of the Road: The Story of the Burma-Shave Signs and Jingles* (Brattleboro, Vermont: Stephen Greene Press, 1965) contains all 600 of the

official jingles which appeared on American highways from 1927 to 1963, when other advertising media replaced them.

[5]Michael Agnes, ed., *Webster's New World College Dictionary* (Foster City, Calif.: IDG Books Worldwide, 2001), 72.

[6]Ibid., 1129.

[7]Ibid., 431.

[8]Ibid., 1118, 84.

[9]Ibid., 1129.

[10]Ibid., 1337.

[11]Ibid., 292.